FRESH MEX

CHEVYS & RIO BRAVO™
FRESH MEX.
COOKBOOK

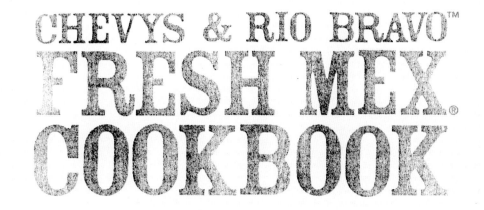

CHEVYS & RIO BRAVO™ FRESH MEX® COOKBOOK

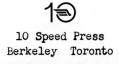

10 Speed Press
Berkeley Toronto

1⊝

10 Speed Press
Box 7123
Berkeley, California 94707
www.tenspeed.com

Cover and book design: Tesser, San Francisco (formerly TreDesign)
Photography: Frankie Frankeny
Food styling: Wesley Martin
Illustrations: Gerry Bustamante and Dennis Ziemienski
Text: Steve Siegelman

Distributed in Australia by Simon & Schuster Australia, in Canada by Ten Speed Press
Canada, in New Zealand by Southern Publishers Group, in South Africa
by Real Books, in Southeast Asia by Berkeley Books, and in the United Kingdom and
Europe by Airlift Books.

Library of Congress Cataloging-in-Publication Data

Chevys and Rio Bravo fresh mex cookbook
    p. cm.
  Includes index.
  ISBN 1-58008-191-6
    1. Mexican American Cookery. 2. Chevys (Restaurant) 3. Rio Bravo (Restaurant)

TX715.2.S69 C49 2000
641.59'26872073--dc21   99-086936

Chevys Fresh Mex®, Fresh Mex®, and El Machino® are registered trademarks of Chevys, Inc.

Printed in China
First printing 2000

1 2 3 4 5 6 7 8 9 10 -- 05 04 03 02 01 00

CONTENTS

our FRESH MEX® PLEDGE

N⁰ 1 We blend fresh salsa every hour!

Our tortilla chips are always fresh! **NO. 2**

#3 We smash fresh avocados daily for guacamole!

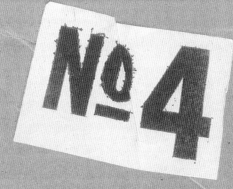

Fish so fresh you'll swear we **caught** it ourselves!

Tortillas **made fresh** off "EL MACHINO®"!

No cans in our **kitchen!**

CHEVYS, RIO BRAVO™ & THE FRESH MEX® REVOLUTION

You sit down. A surprisingly friendly server plunks a big basket of chips and a dish of salsa in front of you. And as you go through the usual drink-ordering and "our-special-today" preliminaries, you absent-mindedly reach for a chip, dip it in the salsa and pop it in your mouth.

Hey! Wait a sec! The chip is warm! It's incredibly thin and crisp. It doesn't taste like the inside of a deep-fryer. And the salsa's spicy and intense, with bits of smoky charred tomato, onions, and jalapeños. It all tastes so...fresh!

WELCOME TO OUR WORLD.

At Chevys and Rio Bravo™, we love watching people try our food for the first time. Because even if they've never heard of "Fresh Mex®," they take one taste and they just get it: Mexican food, carefully made from scratch by real people from really fresh ingredients is unbelievably good. It's light, clean, brightly flavored, and exciting. Or as our customers like to say, "Mmmm!"

We opened our first Chevys in the San Francisco Bay Area back in 1986. It was the height of the "hacienda" era, and Mexican food usually meant soggy enchiladas hidden under a lava flow of melted cheese and sour cream.

We thought we'd throw out all that heavy hacienda-style stuff and start over. Big open dining room. Lots of light. Partitions made out of beer boxes. Fun Latin music. Whopping margaritas in frosty mugs. The fast-paced energy of a border cantina.

Now, when it came to the food, we wanted it to be just as light and exciting as the atmosphere. So we made a commitment: we'd prepare absolutely every single thing from scratch, every day, right in our kitchens—no cans, no week-old vats of beans, no short-cuts. We called our approach Fresh Mex, and we've never looked back.

Over the years, it's dawned on us that Fresh Mex was a pretty revolutionary idea, especially for a restaurant chain. And as we've grown, we've gotten even more fanatical about it. In 1999, we found the perfect partner to join in our crusade—a fun, casual restaurant group called Rio Bravo, based mostly in the Southeast. Together, we've got big plans to share Fresh Mex with the world. And we're starting with you.

THIS BOOK IS YOUR INVITATION TO DISCOVER FRESH MEX® FIRSTHAND, not just by eating at our restaurants, but by trying it yourself in your own kitchen. Let's begin with a look at how we do it in ours.

Fresh Mex®: A Day In The Life

IT'S 5:00 A.M., and Juan Saldoval, the kitchen manager at Chevys, San Francisco, is firing up the coffee maker as he looks over his prep list. The list is pretty much identical to the contents of this book. Imagine making everything on these pages from scratch in just under six hours. For twelve hundred people. That's what Juan and his team do every day.

Juan switches on the radio, and Mexican Top 40s music fills the kitchen. He starts singing along. He's ready to rock 'n' roll.

In quick succession, he meets with the troops and gives them their assignments, laughing and joking in Spanish. Then he checks in 20 cases of tomatoes and another four dozen of lettuce, onions, jalapeños, avocados, mushrooms, bell peppers, and other vegetables.

6:00 The salsa cook hits the ground running. He looks more like a salsa dancer as he whirls between the cutting board, the stove, the steamer and the sink, juggling up to five recipes at a time with perfectly choreographed precision—charring tomatoes and jalapeños in an iron skillet for salsa, braising Salsa Chicken and Carnitas in big open kettles, skillfully cutting up a pork butt for tamales, and whipping up batches of dressing, sauces, and chipotle purée in an enormous blender. He's done this before. You can tell.

Meanwhile, the two veggie prep cooks, who just finished mincing fifty pounds of onions in less than ten minutes, are halving, pitting and scooping out 120 avocados for guacamole.

A few feet away, Isabel, one of two tortilla cooks is working the deep fryer, making everything from hand-cut chips, tostadas and taco shells to individually rolled kiddie cones for ice cream.

7:20 Yolanda, the other tortilla cook has just finished baking corn muffins. Now she's mixing a huge batch of flour tortilla dough and rolling it out into hundreds of dough balls which will be fed into El Machino®, our famous tortilla-making machine.

8:00 All eight cooks are moving at full tilt. Everywhere you look, people are chopping and measuring, tasting and seasoning—cleaning as they go so the kitchen's always spotless.

charring tomatillos for salsa

← the day's produce arrives

making guacamole

8:40 The daily fish order arrives, and Juan checks it for freshness, poking and sniffing his way through the styrofoam boxes. While one of the cooks ices the fish, Juan begins cutting a massive slab of halibut into fillets.

9:15 Antonio, the grill cook, is stacking logs of mesquite charcoal in the grill. As he lights the mesquite, Juan winks and says "even the fire is fresh."

10:00 The sauté and grill stations are coming together, as the cooks bring over their pans of finished sauces, fillings and toppings, fitting them into the stainless steel countertop like pieces in a jigsaw puzzle.

10:45 "Now comes the time when we start getting a little nervous and shaky," says Juan, who started as a dishwasher at Chevys 12 years ago and has worked every station in the kitchen. He's kidding.

Juan grabs a fistful of teaspoons and heads over to the cooking line. This is his moment of truth. He makes his way down the line, tasting every single item—even the sour cream—to make sure it's fresh and properly seasoned. After each taste, he tosses the spoon into the sink behind him and quickly grabs another. He adds a little Pico de Gallo to the beans and some salsa to the rice. Then he whips out a thermometer and checks the temperature of everything on the line, recording it all in his prep log.

IT'S 11:00 Juan looks up, smiling. "We are ready to go," he announces. And that's good news. The first lunch order is just popping out of the printer.

the catch of the day arrives →

rolling tortilla dough

El Machino

DOUGH BALL
INFEED

TORTILLA
DISCHARGE

"the drop"

"the flatten"

"the belt"

"the payoff"

the first lunch order of the day

← fresh sauces and fillings

FRESH MEX. COMES HOME

SO HOW COME WE WROTE THIS COOKBOOK, ANYWAY? Wouldn't we rather just have you come to our place to eat, instead of giving away all our trade secrets? Well, amigo, here's the biggest secret of all. The thing about Fresh Mex is there are no secrets! We wear our philosophy on our sleeves (and sometimes all over our aprons): Keep it fresh. That's about all there is to it.

We think that one simple idea can make a huge difference in the way you cook and eat at home. All you have to do is get up at 5:00 am every day and spend about six hours in the kitchen. Just kidding. It's really as simple as this:

Shop more than once a week, and if you can, buy produce from a produce market or a local farmer's market. Buy meat, poultry and seafood the same day you're going to eat it. Here's a simple rule of thumb: Start by asking what's fresh, then think about how you'd like to cook it.

Raise your right hand and recite our Fresh Mex Pledge No. 6: "No cans in our kitchens. No Way. Nada. Never!" Of course, we're not suggesting that you never buy another can again. The point is, if you're used to buying something Mexican in a can or a jar—like beans or salsa—try making it from scratch. Our step-by-step recipes will tell you how. You'll be amazed at the flavor. We promise.

If there's a half-way decent Mexican section in your supermarket, you'll be able to make most of the recipes in this book. But if there's a Mexican market anywhere near you, check it out anyway. It's fun, and you'll learn a lot. Browse the aisles, ask questions, and buy some stuff you've never tried—like chipotles en adobo, queso fresco, or maybe even a jar of pickled cactus.

Put fresh fruit, vegetables, chiles, and garlic in a nice bowl or basket where you can see them. They look cool, and you'll be more likely to use them.

Jalapeño

Poblano

Habanero

New Mexico

Chipotle dried

Chipotle in adobo

How to Use this Book

This book actually contains oh about 2,867 recipes

THIS BOOK ACTUALLY CONTAINS, OH, ABOUT 2,867 RECIPES.

See, the thing is, Mexican cooking is all about components. We've given you the basic building blocks to make all your favorites from our menus, plus recipes for a bunch of great "specials" our chefs have dreamed up over the years. But you can "Mex and match" those components in an almost infinite number of ways. Make a batch of Salsa Chicken (page 32) on a Sunday afternoon, and you can have burritos, quesadillas, tacos, enchiladas, eggs, pasta, or even just Salsa Chicken all week.

These recipes have been adapted to fit the way real people cook at home. You won't find any mysterious techniques or snobby food jargon. And even though some Fresh Mex dishes may take a little more time (example: soaking beans overnight), you'll find that most of them don't take a whole lot of effort (example: soaking beans overnight).

TWO QUICK TIPS:

BEGIN WITH THE BASICS--Our Fresh Mex Fundamentals chapter is a crash course in the essentials. Start by making beans, rice and salsa. Then work your way through the chapter, trying what sounds interesting. We've provided lots of suggestions for how to use everything.

READ BEFORE YOU LEAP--Almost every recipe in the second, third and fourth chapters has at least one more recipe built into it. We did that on purpose; it's how we cook and how we think about food, and we figured it would make life easier for you. So it's important to make sure you have everything you need, including time, before you start cooking.

Fresh Mex is a philosophy of cooking. But if you've been to Chevys or Rio Bravo, you know that it's also something more. It's fun. Because when we say "fresh" we're not just talking about a perfectly ripe tomato or a beautiful piece of fish. We're talking about a casual, open-minded, unstuffy attitude. We're talking about making party hats out of hollowed-out watermelons.

We hope this book will bring the flavor and fun of Fresh Mex to your table. And in the meantime, we'll always keep a table open for you at our place.

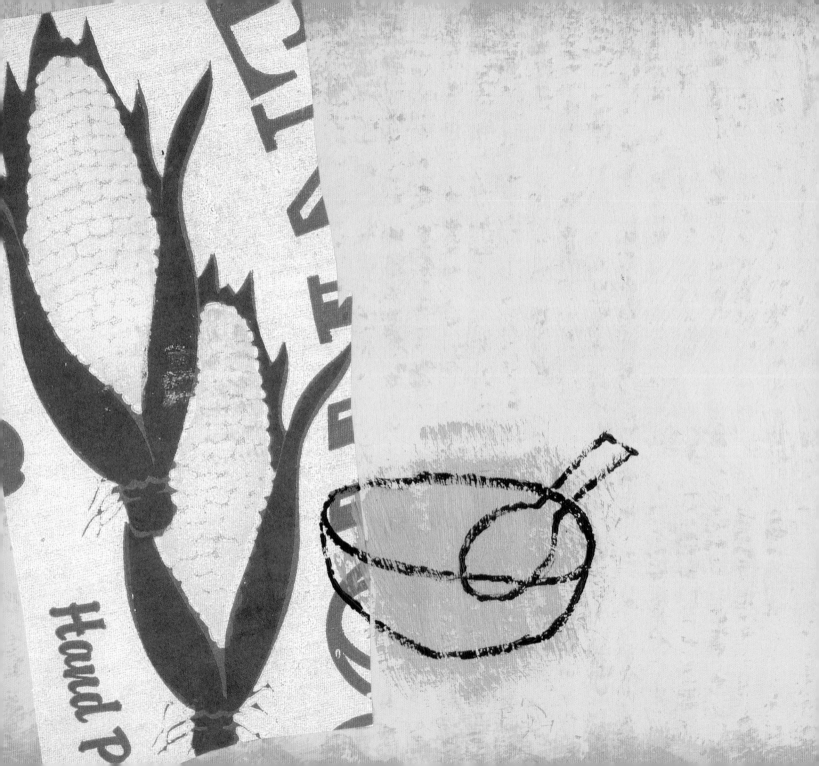

Hand P

FRESh MEX®
FUN-
DAMENTALS

BEANS, RICE, GUACAMOLE & ALL THE FIXIN'S

Tomatillo Salsa Verde

New Mexico Red Chile Sauce

Ranchero Sauce

Fuego Spice Mix

Pickled Jalapeños

Sweet Hot Jalapeño Jelly

Sweet Chipotle Dressing

Chipotle Purée

Roasted Red Pepper and
Chipotle Chile Aioli

Roasted Red Pepper Vinaigrette

Famous Flour Tortillas

Homemade Chicken Stock

Salsa Chicken

Smokin' Chipotle 'Slaw

Rio Bravo Red Rice

Frijoles Refritos

Beans a la Charra

Big-Flavor Black Beans

Sweet Corn Tomalito

Fresh Tortilla Chips

Iron Skillet Tortilla Chips

Tortilla Flats

Everybody's Favorite Guacamole

SALSA AND A SMILE!

Tomatillo Salsa Verde

Makes approximately 2 cups

Use this authentic green salsa as an ingredient in stews and soups, a dip for chips, a sauce for grilled fish and chicken, or a table sauce for everything else (except maybe ice cream). If you've never cooked with tomatillos (the tangy Mexican fruits that look like small green tomatoes with papery husks), this is a good place to start. You can find them fresh in Mexican markets and many supermarkets. They should be firm with tight-fitting husks.

1 pound **tomatillos**, husked

3 **jalapeños**, stemmed, seeded, and cut in half (see **tip**, page 23)

1/2 **onion**, quartered

1/4 teaspoon **ground cumin**

1/4 cup **chopped cilantro**

1/2 teaspoon **salt**

In a stockpot over high heat, boil the tomatillos, jalapeños, and onion in water to cover for 5 minutes. Cook just until al dente, not soft, breaking up the onion quarters as they boil. Drain off the cooking water and transfer the boiled vegetables to a blender or food processor. Add the remaining ingredients and blend until smooth. Store in an airtight container in the refrigerator until ready to use or for up to 3 days.

FRESH MEX TIP #1

Soaking tomatillos in cold water makes it easier to remove their husks.

New Mexico Red Chile Sauce

Makes 6 cups

This earthy red chile sauce is the perfect counterpart to our Tomatillo Salsa Verde, and we use the two like salt and pepper to add flavor to all kinds of dishes. Use this sauce as a condiment, or stir it into stews, soups, and egg dishes. If you're making a batch to keep around, leave out the butter until you're ready to use the sauce.

5 cups **Chicken Stock** (page 32)

1 pound **tomatoes**, quartered

12 ounces **white onions**, quartered

6 cloves **whole peeled garlic**

6 ounces **dried New Mexico chiles**, stemmed and seeded

1 tablespoon **butter**, at room temperature

1 teaspoon **salt**

In a stockpot over high heat, bring the stock, tomatoes, onions, and garlic to a boil. Cook for 15 minutes. Stir the dried chiles into the stock, making sure it covers them. Remove the pan from the heat and soak the chiles for 15 minutes. When the mixture is cool, transfer it to a blender or food processor. Blend until liquefied. Strain through a fine-mesh sieve, pressing on the residue with the back of a ladle to extract all of the chile flavor. In a large saucepan, reheat the sauce and, with a spatula or wooden spoon, stir in the butter until it is melted and incorporated. Stir in the salt. Store in an airtight container in the refrigerator until ready to use or for up to 3 days.

LA CAM
8
LA BOT
46
EL S
2

Huevos Rancheros

Fry a couple of eggs in a small nonstick skillet. Top them with Ranchero Sauce and shredded cheese (such as Cheddar or Jack). Put the pan under the broiler to melt the cheese. Slide the eggs onto a warm flour tortilla and serve with refried beans (page 34).

FRESH MEX TIP #3

HOW TO PEEL, SEED, AND DICE A TOMATO:

1. Remove core
2. Cut an "x" at base
3. Place tomato in boiling water for 10 seconds
4. Cool tomato in ice water
5. Peel off skin with paring knife
6. Cut tomato in half along "equator"
7. Gently squeeze out and discard seeds
8. Slice tomato crosswise into circles.
9. Cut circles into dice.

Ranchero Sauce

Makes 3 cups

This chunky quick-cooked salsa has a lot more flavor than the store-bought stuff. Use it on Chevys Three-Cheese Chile Rellenos (page 76), huevos rancheros, and omelets. Serve it with chips for dipping. Or heat it up and toss it with pasta, just like a traditional Italian tomato sauce (for extra credit, crumble some queso fresco on top).

1 tablespoon olive oil
1 teaspoon minced garlic
3/4 cup chopped onion
3 cups chopped tomatoes
2 teaspoons tomato paste

1 1/2 teaspoons Chipotle Purée (page 26)
1 teaspoon salt
1 teaspoon minced fresh oregano

Heat the oil in a saucepan over medium heat. Add the garlic and onion and sauté until soft. Add the rest of the ingredients, increase the heat to medium-high, and bring to a boil. Once boiling, decrease the heat to low and simmer for 10 minutes. Remove from the heat and let cool. Transfer to an airtight container and refrigerate for up to 3 days. To use, heat slowly over low heat. If necessary, thin with 1 tablespoon of chicken stock (page 32) at a time.

Fuego Spice Mix *Makes 1 cup*

Here's the rub: this fiery spice blend is perfect for seasoning grilled steaks, chops, chicken, and fish. Just rub it on the meat right before cooking. You can add a pinch to sautéed vegetables, too. Or use it to season homemade tortilla chips (page 36), French fries, or popcorn.

1/4 cup paprika

2 teaspoons cayenne

2 tablespoons salt

2 teaspoons ground white pepper

2 tablespoons black pepper

2 tablespoons granulated garlic

2 tablespoons chile powder

2 tablespoons oregano

Combine all ingredients, mixing well. Store in an airtight container, out of direct light, for up to 6 months.

FRESH MEX TIP #4

CHILES: HANDLE WITH CARE

If you haven't had a lot of experience with fresh chiles, here are a few helpful tips.

- Most of the heat in a chile is in the seeds and veins.

- Cooking won't mellow the heat of a chile, only removing seeds and veins will.

- Whatever the size or name of a chile, the only surefire way to judge its fire power is to taste a small piece of the flesh.

- Wear rubber gloves when handling chiles to avoid skin irritation.

- Avoid touching your eyes, mouth, or nose after handling chiles.

Pickled Jalapeños

Makes 2 cups

People used to pickle vegetables all the time as a way of preserving them. At Chevys and Rio Bravo, we still do. We go through hundreds of these fiery little flavor bombs a day, and we put up a fresh batch every morning. We use them as garnishes on salads and entrées, but they're tasty enough to eat right out of the jar (carefully!).

```
2 cups fresh whole jalapeño chiles
  (see tip, page 23)
1/2 cup white vinegar
1/2 cup water
1 teaspoon salt
1 clove raw garlic, sliced
```

Combine all the ingredients in a saucepan over high heat. Bring to a boil, then remove from the heat and let the jalapeños cool in the liquid. Serve the jalapeños when cool, or transfer, along with the cooking liquid, to an air-tight container and store in the refrigerator until ready to use or for up to 1 week.

FRESH MEX TIP #5

An Un-canny Gift Idea

Buy some of those old-time canning jars and fill them with homemade pickled jalapeños or jalapeño jelly. (Follow the directions that come with the jars for safe canning.) Wrap the jars in cornhusks, tie them at the neck with a cornhusk strip. You are so cool.

Sweet Hot Jalapeño Jelly

Makes 3 cups

A restaurant that makes its own jalapeño jelly from scratch? What are we, crazy? Yup. Crazy about fresh, homemade flavor. Actually, this sweet and spicy pepper jelly is quite easy. We serve it with pork fajitas, fish tacos, taquitos, and carnitas, but it also makes a nice dipping sauce for finger food like shrimp or chicken wings.

```
3/4 cup chopped red bell peppers
3/4 cup chopped green bell peppers
1/3 cup diced and seeded jalapeños
  (see tip, page 23)
2 3/4 cups sugar
1/2 cup red wine vinegar
1 tablespoon freshly squeezed lime juice
6 tablespoons Certo liquid pectin
```

Combine the peppers, jalapeños, sugar, vinegar, and lime juice in a large saucepan over medium heat. Heat until warm and sugar is dissolved. Pour the mixture in a blender or food processor and blend for 5 seconds. Return the blended mixture to the saucepan and bring to a boil. Skim off any foam that rises to the surface. Decrease the heat to low and simmer for 5 minutes. Stir in the pectin, increase the heat to medium-high, and bring to a boil. Remove from heat and cool. The jelly will set as it cools down. When cool, cover and refrigerate for up to 5 days.

Makes 2 cups

Sweet Chipotle Dressing

This sweet-hot vinaigrette is the star ingredient in our Smokin' Chipotle 'Slaw. For best flavor, make it a day ahead of time. Tossed with diced mango or pineapple and red onion, it makes a mean fresh salsa. Or use it as a dressing for hearty greens, like romaine or spinach.

```
1 tablespoon diced yellow onion
1 tablespoon chopped garlic
2 tablespoons Dijon mustard
1/4 teaspoon ground cumin
1/2 cup diced fresh tomatoes
2 tablespoons chopped cilantro
2/3 cup seasoned rice wine vinegar
1/4 teaspoon black pepper
1 teaspoon salt
2 tablespoons honey
2 tablespoons Chipotle Purée (see right)
1/2 cup olive oil
```

Place all the ingredients, except the oil, in a blender or food processor, and blend until very smooth. Slowly add the oil, in a thin stream, while the blender or processor is running and blend until all of the oil is incorporated and the vinaigrette is completely emulsified. The vinaigrette will keep for 3 to 5 days in an airtight container.

FRESH MEX TIP #6

Chipotle Purée is an inexact science. It can vary in spiciness from batch to batch (or brand to brand). So, start with a little, then taste and adjust upward.

Makes 1/4 cup

Chipotle Purée

You know that mysterious, smoky, earthy, spicy, just-plain-addictive flavor that you find in so many great Mexican dishes? The flavor you can never quite seem to match at home? This is it. Make up a batch of this incredible stuff, and you'll have instant authenticity any time you want it. Chipotles (chee-pote-lays) are jalapeño chiles that have been slowly dried over smoke. You can find them in Mexican markets, and even in some supermarkets, if you want to make this purée from scratch. But there is an easier way. Buy a can of high-quality chipotles en adobo—chiles marinated in a saucy paste of vinegar and spices—and purée the contents in a blender. This is one of those rare occasions when something from a can tastes just as good as what you'd make from scratch. We can't do it, because of the whole "no cans" thing. But you...uh...can.

```
6 cups water
4 ounces dried chipotle chiles, stems removed
2 tablespoons achiote paste
1 cup tomato paste
1 cup firmly packed brown sugar
1/4 cup red wine vinegar
2 teaspoons salt
1/4 cup olive oil
```

Combine all the ingredients in a saucepan over high heat. Bring the mixture to a boil, decrease heat to medium-low, and simmer for 30 to 45 minutes. Remove from the heat, and cool completely. Purée the mixture in a blender or food processor until smooth. Store in an airtight container in the refrigerator until ready to use or for up to 3 days.

Roasted Red Pepper and Chipotle Chile Aioli

Makes about 1 cup

If you've got roasted peppers around, you can make this creamy spread in a minute. It adds a lot of flavor to burritos, grilled fish, crab cakes, sandwiches, and even burgers. You can also serve it straight up as a dip for fresh vegetables (jicama is particularly good).

```
3 to 4 cloves garlic
Olive oil
1 red bell pepper, roasted, stemmed, and
  seeded (see below)
1 cup mayonnaise
1 teaspoon Chipotle Purée (opposite page)
Juice of 1/2 lemon
1/2 teaspoon salt
```

Preheat the oven to 350°. Place the garlic on a piece of aluminum foil. Drizzle with the olive oil. Roast in the oven for 30 minutes, or until soft. Remove and let cool. Mash with a fork. Combine the roasted garlic and remaining ingredients in a blender or food processor and blend until smooth and creamy. Place in an airtight container and refrigerate until ready to use or for up to 3 days.

Roasted Red Pepper Vinaigrette

Makes 1 1/2 cups

If you're thinking about making an entrée salad (like our Seared Ahi Tuna Salad, page 51), with grilled fish, chicken, or shrimp, this *muy robusto* dressing is the way to go.

```
1/2 cup roasted, peeled, stemmed, seeded,
  and chopped red bell peppers (see below)
1 teaspoon chopped garlic
2 tablespoons chopped onion
2 tablespoons chopped tomato
2 tablespoons red wine vinegar
2 tablespoons freshly squeezed lime juice
1 teaspoon salt
1/2 teaspoon black pepper
1/2 teaspoon Chipotle Purée
  (opposite page), optional
1/2 cup olive oil
```

Place all the ingredients, except the oil, in a blender or food processor, and blend until very smooth. Slowly add the oil, in a thin stream, while the processor is running and blend, until all of the oil is incorporated and the vinaigrette is completely emulsified. Taste and add additional salt if necessary. For a less spicy vinaigrette, omit the Chipotle Purée. Place in an airtight container and refrigerate until ready to use or for up to 3 days.

ROASTED SWEET BELL PEPPERS

Roasting peppers takes a little time, but the smoky flavor you get is worth it. Don't hold back on the charring. The peppers should be black all over. Once they steam, almost all the blackened skin will peel away.

To roast, preheat the broiler. Place the peppers under the hot broiler, turning regularly until all sides are evenly blackened. Place them in a container and cover tightly with plastic wrap. Let the peppers steam for 5 to 10 minutes. Peel or rub the skin off and remove the seeds and stems from the middle of the peppers. Cover tightly and refrigerate until ready to use, or for up to 2 days.

Hot off the Presses: When we opened our first Chevys, we wanted our tortillas to be FRESH--not "fresh today from the factory." Tortillas that were never more than 3 minutes old. Nice idea. Not so easy. Then we discovered El Machino®: the mad-scientist's tortilla-rolling-griddling-and-flipping-while-you-watch machine. Here's how it works: you **drop in a dough ball and 53 seconds later you've got a per-fectly cooked fresh tortilla.** Okay, it's actually more complicated than that--but the bottom line is that just one El Machino cranks out about 1,500 tortillas a day.

WHY WE KEEP EL MACHINO IN THE DINING ROOM

The only trouble when we brought El Machino to the restaurant was that it was too big for la cocina (the kitchen). So, without much thought, we stuck it in the dining room. Wow! Who knew it would be such a hit? Turns out El Machino does more than turn out fantastic tortillas. It's also a side show!

EL MACHINO: tortillas while you watch

Famous Flour Tortillas
Makes 16 8 inch tortillas

Twice a day, we mix up gigantic batches of tortilla dough, divide it into thousands of little balls, and feed them one at a time to El Machino. Here's a slightly scaled-down version.

6 cups all-purpose flour

1 teaspoon baking powder

1/2 teaspoon salt

1/2 cup vegetable shortening, cut into small pieces

2 1/2 cups warm water

Place the flour in the bowl of a mixer and add the baking powder and salt, stirring to mix well. Add the shortening. Turn the mixer on low and slowly pour in the water. Mix on low for 90 seconds or until well mixed.

Scrape the dough out of the bowl onto a floured surface. Divide the dough into 2 equal portions. Cover with plastic wrap and set aside to rest at room temperature for 20 minutes. Divide each half into 8 equal portions. You will now have 16 dough balls. Lightly flour your work surface. With a floured rolling pin, roll each ball into an 8-inch round. Stack the rounds on a baking sheet with plastic wrap between each tortilla. Let the tortillas rest for 10 minutes.

Heat a griddle or large cast-iron skillet over medium heat, and lightly coat with vegetable oil cooking spray. Cook the tortillas on the griddle or in the skillet for 1 minute on each side, or until light brown spots form on the surface.

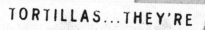

TORTILLAS...THEY'RE

FRESH OR THEY'RE FRISBEES!

EL NOPAL

CANTARIT

Homemade Chicken Stock

Makes 2 quarts

You're thinking, "Why bother?" Two reasons. One: homemade stock is incredibly easy, makes great soups, and makes you feel good. Two: you get to use the chicken in Salsa Chicken (see right). That's why.

1 3- to 4-pound fresh chicken

2 1/2 quarts cold water

1 large celery rib, with leaves, coarsely chopped

1 green onion, top discarded, coarsely chopped

2 carrots, coarsely chopped

1 yellow onion, coarsely chopped

1 bunch cilantro stems

4 to 5 garlic cloves

1/2 teaspoon white pepper

1 teaspoon kosher salt

1 bay leaf

Combine all the ingredients together in a stockpot over high heat. Bring to a boil, then decrease the heat to low and simmer for 1 hour, skimming off any foam or impurities that rise to the surface. Remove from the heat and cool. Remove the chicken, cool, and reserve for another use. Strain off the vegetables and discard. Cover and refrigerate the stock. The next day, remove and discard any fat that has collected on the surface, then use as directed.

Salsa Chicken

Makes about 4 cups

Here's our classic chicken filling for enchiladas, burritos, tacos, quesadillas, tostadas, and flautas.

5 tomatoes, cored and halved

1 jalapeño, stemmed, seeded, and halved (see tip, page 23)

1 yellow onion, peeled and quartered

2 tablespoons olive oil

1 tablespoon minced garlic

2 tablespoons Fuego Spice Mix (page 23)

1 3- to 4-pound cooked chicken (from stock recipe), skinned and meat chopped

1/4 cup chopped cilantro

Preheat the broiler. Place the tomatoes and jalapeño cut-side down in a baking dish. Cut one of the onion halves in half and add to the baking dish. Roast the vegetables under the broiler for 8 to 10 minutes, or until they begin to blacken. Remove from the oven and cool. Transfer the vegetables and accompanying liquid to a blender and pulse until thick and chunky.

Dice the remaining three-quarters of the onion. In a large skillet, heat the olive oil over medium-high heat. Add the onion and garlic and sauté for 5 minutes. Add the spice mix and sauté for 3 to 4 more minutes. Add the chicken pieces, and sauté until the chicken is heated through, stirring often. Add the tomato mixture to the skillet and deglaze, stirring and scraping the bottom of the skillet to loosen any browned bits. Add the cilantro. Bring the mixture to a simmer. Simmer for 10 minutes. Remove from the heat and use as directed.

Smokin´ Chipotle ´Slaw

Serves 6

This 'slaw is perfect in fish tacos (page 70) or as a side dish with grilled meats, but you might just want to scarf it down with a sandwich.

3 cups finely shredded white cabbage
3 cups finely shredded red cabbage
3/4 cup Sweet Chipotle Dressing (page 26)

In a large mixing bowl, combine the cabbage. Toss gently with the dressing to combine.

Rio Bravo Red Rice

Makes 4 cups

If you love fluffy, restaurant-style Mexican red rice, here's how it's done. You can serve it with, in, on, or under just about anything in this book.

6 beefsteak or 8 plum tomatoes
1 tablespoon chopped cilantro
2 cups water
1 teaspoon chopped garlic
2 teaspoons Chipotle Purée (page 26)
2 teaspoons salt
1/3 cup canola oil
2 cups long-grain white rice
1/2 cup chopped yellow onion

In a heavy skillet over medium-high heat, place the tomatoes and char until their skins split and they become aromatic. Transfer the tomatoes to a blender or food processor and purée. Stir in the cilantro. Set aside.

In a large saucepan, combine the water, puréed tomatoes, garlic, Chipotle Purée, and salt. Bring to a boil. Heat the oil in another large saucepan over high heat until just before the oil begins to smoke. Add the rice and onion and sauté until three-quarters of the grains are bright white or slightly brown, 7 to 10 minutes. (Do not drain the oil.) Add the tomato mixture from the other saucepan, and simmer for 15 minutes. Remove the rice from the heat, cover, and let stand covered 20 to 30 minutes, stirring every 10 minutes and tasting to see whether the rice is done. When the rice is cooked through, fluff with a fork, then keep warm until ready to serve.

LA BOTELL

EL NOPAL

EL CAZO

FRIJOLES REFRITOS

Makes about 3 cups

3 tablespoons solid vegetable shortening
1/2 cup chopped yellow onion
4 cups Beans a la Charra (opposite page), with cooking
   liquid

Heat the shortening in a heavy-bottomed pan over high heat until almost
smoking. Add the onions and sauté until clear, approximately 3 minutes.
Add the beans to the sauté pan and mash until about two-thirds of the
beans are mashed and one-third is still whole.

Beans a la Charra

Makes 8 cups

These "cowboy beans" have been on our menu right from the start. They're tender pintos, simmered with bacon and jalapeños, and they cook up nice and soupy. In fact, you can even serve them as a soup by puréeing some of the beans and stirring them back in.

3 cups dried pinto beans

3 quarts water

6 slices (about 8 ounces) uncooked bacon, coarsely chopped

1/2 cup diced onion

1 tablespoon chopped garlic

1/2 jalapeño, stemmed, seeded, and chopped (see tip, page 23)

1 tablespoon chile powder

2 teaspoons ground cumin

1 tablespoon salt

In a stockpot, soak the beans overnight in the water (to cover). The next day, cook the bacon in a skillet over medium-high heat until crisp, about 6 to 8 minutes. Add the onion, garlic, and jalapeño and cook for 5 minutes. Stir in the chile powder and cumin and cook for 1 minute more. Add 1 cup of the soaking water from the beans while stirring and scraping the bottom of the skillet to loosen all the brown bits adhered to the pan. Add the beans and remaining water, and bring to a rapid boil. Decrease the heat to medium-low, and simmer for 1 1/2 to 2 hours, or until the beans are soft. When the beans are cooked through, add the salt, and cook 1 to 2 more minutes. Keep warm until ready to serve, or cool, cover, and refrigerate for up to 3 days.

Big-Flavor Black Beans

Makes about 6 cups

Beans can be bland. But not these beans. They're spicy and satisfying. Make extra, and you can serve them as black bean soup. Just thin with a little water or stock and stir in some Pico de Gallo (page 48) or Fiesta Salsa (page 51).

2 cups dried black beans

3 quarts water

3/4 cup yellow onions, cut into 3/8-inch diced cubes

1 tablespoon chopped garlic

1 tablespoon ground cumin

2 teaspoons chile powder

1 teaspoon Chipotle Purée (page 26)

1/3 cup ketchup

1 teaspoon dried oregano

2 teaspoons salt

In a stockpot, soak the beans overnight in the water (to cover). The next day, add the remaining ingredients, except the salt. Bring to a boil and stir. Decrease the heat to medium, cover, and simmer until the beans are slightly firm in the middle yet tender, about 1 1/2 to 2 hours. If the liquid evaporates before the beans are cooked, add more water 1/4 cup at a time. When the beans are cooked through, add the salt and cook 1 to 2 more minutes. Keep warm until ready to serve, or cool, cover, and refrigerate for up to 3 days.

Sweet Corn Tomalito

serves 4 to 6

Here's that wildly popular sweet corn pudding that shows up as a little side dish on a lot of our combos. If you can't get good fresh corn, use frozen corn, thawed and drained.

```
6 cups fresh corn kernels
3/4 cup milk
1/4 cup (1/2 stick) butter
1/2 cup prepared masa for tamales
  (see note, below)
2/3 cup sugar
3/4 cup cornmeal
3/4 teaspoon baking powder
3/4 teaspoon salt
1/4 cup milk
```

Preheat the oven to 250°. Blend 3 cups of corn kernels and the milk in a blender or food processor until smooth. Whip the butter, masa, and sugar together in the food processor until light and fluffy, about 2 minutes. Add all ingredients, including the puréed corn and the remaining 3 cups whole corn kernels, and mix well. Pour the mixture into a 9 x 13-inch pan. Cover tightly with aluminum foil. Set the pan in a large roasting pan. Pour enough cool water into the roasting pan to reach 3/4 inch up the outside of the 9 x 13-inch pan. Bake for 1 1/2 to 2 hours, or until the corn mixture registers 175° on an instant-read thermometer and the corn mixture is set. Scoop out portions of the pudding and serve hot.

NOTE : If fresh masa is not available (see page 80), use masa harina and adjust the ratio of dry masa to milk (liquid) as directed on the package.

Fresh Tortilla Chips

Makes about 3 dozen

We're famous for our chips for a simple reason. They're made fresh every day from hand-cut corn tortillas, and they're served warm. Next time you're in the store and find yourself reaching for a bag of chips, grab a package of tortillas instead and give these a try.

```
Canola oil
8 6-inch corn tortillas, cut into wedges
Salt
```

Line a baking sheet with paper towels. Fill a heavy-bottomed skillet with 3 inches of oil. Heat the oil over high heat until it registers 350° on a candy thermometer. Drop one small handful of tortilla wedges into the oil and cook for 45 seconds or until chips are crisp and deep gold in color, moving them around with tongs to ensure even cooking and prevent them from sticking together. Remove with a wire-mesh strainer, and transfer to the paper towel–lined baking sheet to drain. Salt generously. Repeat until all wedges are fried. Serve warm.

Makes about 4 handfuls

Iron Skillet Tortilla Strips

A little tangle of crispy tortilla strips adds a lot of drama and texture to soups and salads. To make them, cut six 6-inch tortillas into 1/8-inch strips. Follow the directions for frying chips.

TORTILLA FLATS

To make the world's best nachos (page 64) or an edible "plate" for tostada salads, fry whole corn tortillas one at a time, as directed for the chips and strips but using 1- to 2-inch-deep oil, flipping once during cooking. Drain flat on paper towels.

Fresh Mex® Avocados

AM🥑LE

BRAND · EST. 1942

GUAC THIS WAY!

PICKED FRESH

Everybody's Favorite Guacamole

Makes 2 cups

Want to know the secret of great guacamole? Less is more. Forget about the chili powder, the salsa from a jar, the half-pint of sour cream. Just keep it fresh and simple, and when people ask you, "What makes this so good?" Just smile mysteriously and say, "Less than you think."

```
3 avocados (Haas medium)
1 tablespoon freshly squeezed lime juice
1/2 cup Pico de Gallo (page 48)
1 1/2 teaspoon chopped garlic
1 teaspoon olive oil
1 teaspoon stemmed, seeded, and minced jalapeño
  (see tip, page 23)
1 teaspoon salt
```

Pit the avocados. Score avocado meat without cutting through the skin. Scoop out the avocado meat with a large spoon and place in mixing bowl. Add the lime juice, and stir to evenly coat the avocados. Stir in the Pico de Gallo, garlic, oil, jalapeño, and salt, gently mashing and tossing the avocado pieces. The guacamole is the right consistency when more large pieces than mashed parts remain. Do not overmash.

FRESH MEX TIP #8

Jicama "Chips"

Cut fresh jicama into 1/8" thick "chips" and serve with guacamole as a fat-free alternative to tortilla chips.

FRESH MEX TIP #9

HOW TO PREP AN AVOCADO:

1. Slice avocado lengthwise around pit and twist halves apart.

2. Carefully strike pit with blade of a sharp knife. Use knife to twist out pit.

3. Score avocado without cutting through skin.

4. Scoop out meat with large spoon.

FRESh STARTS

SALSA, DRINKS & APPETIZERS

Strawberry-Banana Margarita

Original Frozen Margarita

Mango Margarita

Melonball Tequini

The Perfect Diez Tequini

Sea of Cortez Tequini

Grilled Pineapple Salsa

Mucho Mango Salsa

Fresh Mex Tomatillo Salsa

Pico de Gallo

Corn and Pepper Pico

Green Apple Salsa Fresca

Seared Ahi Tuna Salad

Fiesta Salsa

Mexican Caesar Salad

Red Chile Chicken Taquitos

Wings O' Fire

Parmesan-Crusted Dungeness
Crab Quesadillas

Shrimp Ceviche

Yucatán Chicken Skewers

Fajita Nachos

Fresh Mex® Margaritas

Want to build a better margarita? Say nix to the mix and make 'em like we do with fresh fruit juices and purées. Here are three of our finest.

LA SANDIA

CANTARIT

STRAWBERRY-BANANA MARGARITA *Serves 1*

Kinda like a smoothie. Only more fun!

9 ounces Frozen Margarita (see right)
1/2 banana
1 1/2 ounces Fresh Strawberry Purée
  (see below)
1 fresh strawberry
1 thin lime slice

In a blender, blend the strawberry purée, banana, and Frozen Margarita just until slushy and well mixed. Pour the margarita into the mug, garnish with the strawberry and and lime slice, and serve.

ORIGINAL FROZEN MARGARITA *Serves 1*

There are only three places in the world where you can find the perfect frozen margarita: Chevys, Rio Bravo, and now, your blender.

Kosher salt
About 1 1/2 cups crushed ice
4 ounces Fresh Sweet and Sour Mix (see below)
1 1/4 ounces tequila
1/2 ounce Triple Sec
1 thin lime slice

Salt the rim of a 12-ounce frosted mug. Combine the tequila, Triple Sec, sweet and sour mix, and ice in a blender. Blend just until slushy and well mixed. Pour the margarita into the mug, garnish with the lime slice, and serve.

MANGO MARGARITA *Serves 1*

This is our most requested fresh fruit margarita—which is why we always keep plenty of fresh mangoes in stock.

9 ounces Frozen Margarita (recipe above)
3 ounces Fresh Mango Purée (see left)
2 thin lime slices

In a blender, blend the Frozen Margarita and mango purée just until slushy and well mixed. Pour the margarita into the mugs, garnish with the lime slices, and serve.

FRESH MEX MIXERS

Makes 16 ounces

FRESH SWEET AND SOUR MIX: Combine 1 1/4 cup freshly squeezed lime juice, 2/3 cup freshly squeezed lemon juice, and 2/3 cup sugar in a blender. Blend until the sugar dissolves.

Makes 16 ounces

FRESH MANGO PURÉE: Peel and cut the flesh away from the pits of 2 to 3 mangoes. Place the flesh in a blender or food processor and blend until puréed and smooth.

Makes about 12 ounces

FRESH STRAWBERRY PURÉE: Wash and stem 12 ounces very ripe strawberries. Combine the strawberries and 2 tablespoons sugar in a blender and blend until puréed and smooth.

Margarita
BRAND

GET FRESH at CHEVYS™

BIGGER MARGARITAS

HAPPIER HOUR!

Pictured: Mango Margarita

FRESH MEX TIP #10

To salt or sugar a glass, rub a piece of lime around the rim, then dip it in a plate of kosher salt or sugar.

Fresh Mex® Tequinis™

What would you say to a Mexican martini made with premium tequila? Say what we say. Say "teh-kee-nee." (Rhymes with bikini.)

MELONBALL TEQUINI *Serves 1*

Here's our signature "Mexican Martini" made with a refreshing splash of melon liqueur.

Sugar

Ice cubes

2 ounces Fresh Sweet and Sour Mix (page 42)

1 1/2 ounces Cuervo Gold tequila

1/2 ounce Midori liqueur

1 thin lime slice

Sugar the rim of a martini glass. Fill a shaker half full with the ice. Add the tequila, sweet and sour mix, and Midori. Shake vigorously 15 times. Strain the drink into the glass. Shake the shaker once more, and strain again, adding the remaining drops to the glass.

THE PERFECT DIEZ TEQUINI *Serves 1*

"Diez," as in "ten." Which is what you'll rate this super-smooth concoction of fine tequila and Triple Sec.

Ice cubes

2 ounces Fresh Sweet and Sour Mix (page 42)

1 1/2 ounces Herradura Gold tequila

1/4 ounce Triple Sec

1/2 ounce freshly squeezed orange juice

1 thin lime slice

Continued...

Fill a shaker half full with the ice. Add the tequila, sweet and sour mix, Triple Sec, and orange juice. Shake vigorously 15 times. Strain the drink into a martini glass. Shake the shaker once more, and strain again, adding the remaining drops to the glass. Garnish with the lime slice.

SEA OF CORTEZ TEQUINI *Serves 1*

Wash the blues away with this elegant sapphire-colored cocktail.

Ice cubes

2 ounces Fresh Sweet and Sour Mix (page 42)

1 1/2 ounces Herradura Silver

1/2 ounce Blue Curaçao

1 twist of lemon peel

Fill a shaker half full with the ice. Add the tequila, sweet and sour mix, and Blue Curaçao. Shake vigorously 15 times. Strain the drink into a martini glass. Shake the shaker once more, and strain again, adding the remaining drops to the glass. Garnish with the lemon twist.

Fresh Mex® SALSA Brand

BLENDED FRESH

BLENDED HOURLY RIGHT HERE !

Grilled Pineapple Salsa
Makes about 4 cups

The next time you've got the grill going, give this recipe a shot. Grilling caramelizes some of the sugar in the pineapple and gives it a nice smoky flavor. This salsa will go with just about anything else you decide to grill.

1 ripe pineapple

1 large red bell pepper, roasted, peeled, and diced into 1/4-inch pieces (page 27)

2 tablespoons freshly squeezed lime juice

1/4 cup chopped cilantro

1/2 teaspoon salt

Pinch of ground black pepper

1 to 2 tablespoons Chipotle Purée (page 26)

Start the coals in a charcoal grill or preheat a gas grill. Cut away the pineapple skin, but do not core the pineapple. Slice the pineapple into 1/4-inch-thick rings and grill for 2 to 3 minutes per side, or until crisscross grill marks appear on both sides. The grill marks should be a deep brown color, not black. Remove from the grill and set aside to cool. When cool, dice the grilled pineapple rings into 1/4-inch pieces, cutting away the core as you dice. Combine all the ingredients, except the Chipotle Purée, in a mixing bowl and mix thoroughly to blend the flavors. Add the purée 1 teaspoon at a time, until the salsa is as spicy as you like. Serve chilled.

Mucho Mango Salsa
Makes 1 1/2 to 2 cups

Sweet and tangy with a blast of fiery habanero heat. Try it in grilled fish tacos, serve it with Carnitas (page 82), or toss a little in a mixed green salad with sliced avocado.

1 large mango, peeled, seeded, and diced

1/4 cup finely diced red onion

1 1/2 teaspoons minced cilantro

1 teaspoon freshly squeezed lime juice

1/2 teaspoon minced habanero (see tip, page 23)

2 tablespoons finely diced red bell pepper

1/4 teaspoon salt

Combine all ingredients, mixing well. Serve chilled.

FRESH MEX TOMATILLO SALSA
Makes 2 cups

Looking for a dip for tortilla chips? This spicy salsa is the one to beat.

1 pound tomatillos, husked

1/2 onion, quartered

10 jalapeños, stemmed

1 rounded tablespoon chopped garlic

3/4 cup chopped cilantro

1/4 cup Chipotle Pureé (page 26)

1 rounded tablespoon salt

1 tablespoon freshly squeezed lime juice

Preheat the broiler. Place the tomatillos, onion quarters, and jalapeños in a baking dish. Roast the vegetables under the broiler for 8 to 10 minutes, or until they begin to blacken. Remove from the oven and cool. When cool, transfer the vegetables, and any liquid that has seeped out, along with the rest of the ingredients to a blender or food processor and pureé. Serve chilled.

Pico de Gallo

Makes 2 cups

It's the poster child of Fresh Mex. Use this bright, fresh tomato-jalapeño salsa as a garnish to add color, flavor, texture, spice, and a refreshing coolness all at the same time! Quick, easy, and great as a chip dip, too.

```
2 cups (1 pound) tomatoes, diced into 3/8-
  inch pieces
1/2 cup white onions, diced
2 tablespoons chopped cilantro
1 1/2 tablespoons stemmed, seeded, and
  minced jalapeño (see tip, page 23)
2 teaspoons freshly squeezed lime juice
1/2 teaspoon salt
```

Combine all ingredients, mixing well. Serve chilled.

Corn and Pepper Pico

Makes 2 1/2 cups

Make this good-looking, no-cooking relish in the summer when fresh sweet corn is at its peak. Perfect for grilled fish or chicken. Or stir it into Rio Bravo Red Rice (page 33) for extra color and crunch.

```
1 cup fresh corn kernels
1 cup finely diced red bell peppers
1/2 cup finely diced red onions
1 tablespoon chopped cilantro
1 1/2 teaspoons freshly squeezed lime juice
1 1/2 teaspoons Chipotle Purée (page 26)
1/2 teaspoon salt
```

Combine all ingredients, mixing well. Serve chilled.

Green Apple Salsa Fresca

Makes 3 cups

Crisp green apples and fresh green chiles were meant for each other, and their flavors are fantastic with pork or salmon. Serve this salsa with pork fajitas (page 104), or warm it quickly in a sauté pan and spoon it over slices of roast pork or lamb.

```
1/4 cup apple juice
2 cups peeled, cored, and diced green
  apples
1/2 cup chopped red onions
1/2 cup seeded and diced fresh poblano
  chiles (see tip, page 23)
1/2 teaspoon minced fresh oregano
1 tablespoon sugar
1 tablespoon freshly squeezed lime juice
1 tablespoon seasoned rice wine vinegar
```

Combine all ingredients, mixing well. Serve chilled.

Pictured: Green Apple Salsa Fresca (left), Fiesta Salsa (right) Page 51

Beach Resort

SAN
LUCA

FISH SO FRESH
IT SHOULD BE SLAPPED

Seared Ahi Tuna Salad *Serves 6*

Hold the mayo! This tuna salad's got a whole new attitude. It's made with slices of seared tuna on a bed of greens tossed with a tangy Red Pepper Vinaigrette, and it's a lot easier than it looks. Sear the tuna ahead of time and slice it at the last minute. If you're not a tuna lover, grilled chicken or shrimp work great, too.

2 tablespoons olive oil

1 1/2 pounds sushi-quality tuna, split into steaks, about 1 1/2 to 2 inches thick

1/4 cup Fuego Spice Mix (page 23)

1 pound salad mix, rinsed and dried

3/4 cups Roasted Red Pepper Vinaigrette (page 27)

1 cup Mucho Mango Salsa (page 47)

1 cup Fiesta Salsa (recipe follows)

1 cup roasted red pepper strips (page 27)

1 cup grated queso fresco

Tortilla strips (page 36)

6 cilantro sprigs

TO MAKE THE SALAD: Heat the olive oil in a skillet over high heat until smoking. Coat both sides of the tuna with the spice mix and place in the pan. Sear the tuna on all sides. Let cool, then refrigerate. Transfer the tuna to a cutting board and slice into thin strips. Place the salad mix in a large mixing bowl and toss with the vinaigrette to coat evenly.

TO SERVE: Divide the salad among 6 chilled salad bowls. Arrange the tuna strips in a "teepee" fashion over the lettuce. Sprinkle the Mucho Mango and Fiesta salsas over the salads. Place the roasted bell pepper strips between the tuna strips. Sprinkle the queso fresco and tortilla strips over the top. Garnish each with a cilantro sprig.

FIESTA SALSA
Makes 2 cups

1/3 cup diced jicama

1/3 cup diced red bell pepper

1/4 cup diced red onions

1/4 cup diced green bell peppers

1/3 cup diced celery

1/3 cup fresh whole corn kernels

1/2 cup drained and rinsed Big-Flavor Black Beans (page 35)

1/4 cup Sweet Chipotle Dressing (page 26)

1/4 teaspoon salt

Gently combine all ingredients, mixing well. Serve chilled.

Mexican Caesar Salad

Serves 4

Technically speaking, Caesar salad is already Mexican. It was invented by a guy named Caesar Cardini at his Tijuana restaurant in the '20s. But let's just say our version is a little more Mexican, thanks to the Fajita Chicken, tortilla strips, and queso fresco. We think Caesar would approve.

1 large head romaine lettuce

3 cups Chile-Rubbed Chicken Fajita meat (page 97), cooled and cut into 1/2-inch strips

Iron-Skillet Tortilla Strips (page 36)

Caesar Dressing (recipe follows)

1 cup julienned roasted red peppers, stemmed, peeled, and seeded (page 27)

4 ounces queso fresco

4 cilantro sprigs

Trim the lettuce leaves. Cut into 1-inch pieces, and then wash and dry them thoroughly. In a large mixing bowl, toss with the chicken, tortilla strips, and dressing. Divide among 4 serving bowls. Top with the bell pepper, cheese, and cilantro. Serve immediately.

CAESAR DRESSING

Makes about 1 1/4 cups

1/2 cup mayonnaise

1/2 teaspoon chopped garlic

1/4 cup chopped cilantro

1/4 cup chopped green onion

1/2 teaspoon salt

1 teaspoon black pepper

1/4 cup freshly squeezed lime juice

3 anchovy fillets

1 tablespoon Dijon mustard

1/4 cup queso fresco

Combine 2 tablespoons of the mayonnaise and the remaining ingredients in a blender or food processor. Blend until mixed. Transfer to a mixing bowl. Whisk in the remaining mayonnaise, blending well. Cover and refrigerate until ready to use.

THE CASE FOR QUESO

If Mexican cheeses are available in your supermarket or a local Mexican market, give them a try. Their mild, fresh taste is just right with the bold, earthy flavors of Mexican cooking.

- Queso fresco ("fresh cheese") is soft, white, and crumbly. It's often sprinkled on foods as a garnish. Queso fresco is usually sold in plastic tubs. Substitute farmer cheese or feta.

- Queso añejo ("aged cheese," also called cotija), also great for grating and sprinkling, is drier and firmer than queso fresco and resembles Parmesan, which can be used as a substitute.

- Melting cheeses, such as Chihuahua, are shredded and melted on top of foods or added to fillings. Substitute jack, mild Cheddar, or a blend of the two.

Red Chile Chicken Taquitos *Serves 4*

A guaranteed crowd-pleaser: crispy rolled taquitos with a succulent chicken filling. Our foolproof skewer-frying technique makes them easy.

16 chipotle-flavored or unflavored
  corn tortillas

Salsa Chicken, cold and drained
  of juices (page 32)

Sweet Hot Jalapeño Jelly (page 24)

Grilled Pineapple Salsa (page 47)

1/2 cup queso fresco

4 cilantro sprigs

Chipotle Sour Cream (page 71)

TO MAKE THE TAQUITOS: Preheat the oven to 375°. On a baking sheet, place 4 of the tortillas in the oven for 3 to 4 minutes. Remove from the oven. (This will soften the tortillas so that they won't crack when filled.) Alternatively, warm the tortillas for 30 seconds in the microwave. Set the tortillas on your work surface and spoon about 1/4 cup of the chicken in a line down the center. Roll up into tight cylinders and set parallel to one another on the work surface. Cut four 10-inch skewers in half. Insert one-half of the skewer through one end of four rolls to hold together. Insert another skewer half through the other end of the same rolls. Do not press the skewered rolls too close to one another. Repeat for the other three sets of four rolls.

Line a platter with paper towels. Fill a heavy-bottomed skillet with 3 inches of oil. Heat over high heat until oil registers 350° on an instant-read kitchen thermometer. Place one set of four skewered rolls into the hot oil and deep-fry for 2 to 3 minutes, or until crisp. Remove with tongs and transfer to the paper towel-lined platter to drain.

TO SERVE: Spoon a small mound of jelly in the center of each plate. Spoon another mound of salsa next to the jelly. Remove the skewers from the taquitos, cut in half on the bias and fan out around the jelly and salsa. Sprinkle the cheese over the taquitos and garnish with the cilantro. Put the sour cream sauce in a squirt bottle and make zigzags over the plate to decorate.

EL RANCH-O DRESSING
Makes 2 1/2 cups

1 cup buttermilk

1 tablespoon freshly
squeezed lime juice

1 tablespoon minced cilantro

1 teaspoon minced fresh
oregano

1 tablespoon finely diced
yellow onion

2 teaspoons minced garlic

1/2 teaspoon salt

2 teaspoons black pepper

1 1/2 cups cold mayonnaise

Combine the buttermilk, lime juice, cilantro, oregano, onion, garlic, salt, and pepper, whisking until combined. Add the mayonnaise and whisk until smooth. Cover and refrigerate for 1 hour to develop flavors. The dressing will keep for up to 1 week in an airtight container.

Wings O´ Fire   *serves 6 to 8*

This recipe makes a big batch for a big crowd. The two-step cooking method seals in the spices and turns out some of the juiciest wings you'll ever taste. Serve them with El Ranch-O Dressing or Chipotle Sour Cream (page 71).

```
1/2 cup olive oil

1 cup Fuego Spice Mix (page 23)

5 pounds chicken drumettes

1 1/2 cups Blazin' BBQ Sauce
  (see recipe right)

6 sprigs cilantro

2 1/2 cups El Ranch-O Dressing
  (opposite page)
```

TO MAKE THE WINGS: Mix the oil and spice mix in a large mixing bowl. Add the chicken wings and toss until each piece is fully coated. Preheat the oven to 350°. Place the wings in a large baking pan and bake for 30 minutes, or until an instant-read thermometer inserted in the meat reads 165° or higher. Cool the wings, then cover and refrigerate until ready to finish preparing and serve.

TO GRILL THE WINGS: Prepare the coals in a charcoal grill or preheat a gas grill. When the coals are hot, grill the wings until heated through, turning continually as they cook, about 4 minutes. Transfer the grilled wings to a large mixing bowl, add the BBQ sauce, and toss until the wings are completely coated. Transfer the wings to a serving platter. Garnish with the cilantro and serve with the dressing for dipping.

Makes 2 cups

BLAZIN' BBQ SAUCE

```
2 tablespoons olive oil

1/2 cup chopped yellow onion

2 tablespoons minced garlic

1 teaspoon ground cumin

1 tablespoon dark chile powder

1/3 cup malt vinegar

1 cup ketchup

3/4 cup firmly packed dark brown sugar

1/4 cup dark soy sauce

2 tablespoons L&P Worcestershire sauce

2 tablespoons Chipotle Purée (page 26)
```

TO MAKE THE SAUCE: Heat the oil in a saucepan over medium heat. Add the onion, garlic, cumin, and chile powder and sauté until the onions are soft. Add the malt vinegar and deglaze, stirring and scraping the bottom of the saucepan to loosen all the brown bits adhered to the pan. Add the rest of the ingredients and simmer until slightly thickened. Transfer to a blender or food processor, and blend until smooth. Place in an airtight container and refrigerate until ready to use or for up to 3 days.

Parmesan-Crusted Dungeness Crab Quesadillas

Serves 4

When you've got a little extra time to spend in the kitchen, give these crispy quesadillas stuffed with an unbelievable creamy crab filling a try. They're totally worth the effort. And by the way, check out our patented Parmesan-on-the-outside technique. It'll give any kind of quesadilla a golden, crunchy crust.

1 tablespoon plus 2 teaspoons olive oil

1/2 cup diced onion

1 teaspoon minced garlic

1/2 cup stemmed, seeded, and diced red peppers

1/2 cup chopped green onions

1/2 cup Chipotle-Cream Cheese Sauce (page 75)

8 ounces Dungeness crabmeat

Salt and pepper

4 12-inch flour tortillas

1/4 cup grated Parmesan

1 cup grated Monterey jack

1 cup crumbled queso fresco

Roasted Red Pepper and Chipotle Chile Aioli (page 27)

Mucho Mango Salsa (page 47)

1/4 cup chopped cilantro

TO MAKE THE FILLING: Heat 1 tablespoon of the olive oil in a saucepan over medium-high heat. Add the onion and sauté until clear. Add the garlic, red peppers, and green onions and sauté for 30 seconds, or until soft. Add the Chipotle-Cream Cheese Sauce and bring to a boil. Remove from heat and fold in crabmeat. Season to taste with salt and pepper.

TO MAKE THE QUESADILLAS: Preheat a griddle or heat a large skillet over medium heat. Lay one tortilla on the work surface. Brush the top side of the tortilla with 1/2 teaspoon of the remaining olive oil. Sprinkle 1 tablespoon of the Parmesan over the tortilla. Carefully flip the tortilla, oil-and-cheese-side down, onto the griddle or skillet. Spread the top with 1/4 cup of the jack cheese, 1/4 cup of the queso fresco, and one-quarter of the crab filling over the tortilla, leaving a 1/2-inch border around the edge. Cook the quesadilla for 4 to 5 minutes, or until the cheese is melted and the other side is golden brown. Place the quesadilla on the work surface and fold in half. Repeat with the remaining tortillas and filling to make the other 3 quesadillas.

TO SERVE: Cut the quesadillas into wedges and place on serving plates. Place the aioli in a squirt bottle and decorate the plates with a zigzag pattern, or alternatively, spoon over the quesadillas. Spoon the salsa on the quesadillas and sprinkle with the chopped cilantro.

Shrimp Ceviche

Hot day? Company coming over? We've got one word for you: ceviche. It's a traditional Mexican appetizer made with chunks of fresh fish or seafood marinated in lime juice. The acidic marinade actually "cooks" the protein in the fish in the same way heat does, turning it firm and opaque.

1 pound fresh rock shrimp or prawns, peeled, deveined, and chopped into 1/2-inch chunks

1/2 cup fresh squeezed lime juice

1/4 teaspoon salt

1/4 teaspoon white pepper

1/2 cup finely julienned red bell peppers

1/2 cup finely julienned red onions

1/4 cup stemmed, seeded, and finely julienned poblano peppers (see tip, page 23)

1 cup fresh corn kernels

1/4 cup chopped cilantro

1 teaspoon Chipotle Pureé (page 26)

1 1/2 teaspoons sugar

1/2 cup seasoned rice wine vinegar

1/2 cup julienned yellow bell peppers

1/4 cup thin rings of stemmed and seeded wax peppers, plus additional for garnish (see tip, page 23)

1/2 cup seeded julienned plum tomatoes

1 head radicchio, leaves washed and dried, optional

1 avocado, thinly sliced

6 sprigs cilantro

TO MAKE THE CEVICHE: In a mixing bowl, combine the shrimp, lime juice, salt, and white pepper. Stir gently to mix well. Cover and marinate in the refrigerator for 12 hours. The shrimp will be bright pink and firm all the way through when fully "cooked" by the lime juice marinade. To test for doneness, remove one shrimp and cut open with a knife. If the shrimp are not ready, marinate them for 1 more hour, then retest, repeating until they appear done. Completely drain.

TO SERVE: Transfer the marinated shrimp to a serving bowl. Add the remaining ingredients, except the radicchio, avocado, and cilantro, and stir gently to mix well. Place a few leaves of radicchio on each plate. Divide the ceviche among the plates. Garnish with the avocado, cilantro, and additional wax pepper rings. Serve immediately.

FRESH MEX TIP #12

BUY SEAFOOD FOR CEVICHE from a clean, reputable source; specify that you'll be using it in ceviche to ensure that you get the freshest stuff.

SNAPPER OR SCALLOPS also make great Ceviche. Whatever you use, make sure to start with only the freshest fish or shellfish.

INSTANT UPGRADE: serve ceviche in a martini glass with a salted rim (page 44).

FRESH MEX FISH AND CHIPS Garnish Ceviche with a few tortilla chips or strips (page 36) for a nice texture contrast.

Yucatán Chicken Skewers *serves 4*

If there's a perfect party food, it's got to be grilled skewers. They're easy to make and nobody can resist them. These are particularly mouthwatering, especially when you serve them with Mucho Mango Salsa (page 47), Green Apple Salsa Fresca (page 48) or Fiesta Salsa (page 51). If you're feeling really festive, go wild and serve the skewers impaled in a halved pineapple with Grilled Pineapple Salsa (page 47) on the side.

4 12-inch-long stainless steel or bamboo skewers

1 pound boneless, skinless chicken breast, cut into 2-inch pieces

1 1/2 cups Yucatan Marinade (see below)

TO MAKE THE SKEWERS: If using bamboo skewers, soak overnight in water. Thread the chicken pieces on the skewers lengthwise, covering as much of the skewers as possible. Place the skewers in a roasting pan or other large container and fully cover with marinade. Cover and marinate overnight in the refrigerator.

TO GRILL THE SKEWERS: The next day, start the coals in a charcoal grill or preheat a gas grill. When the coals are hot, remove the chicken skewers from the marinade, discard the marinade, and grill the chicken in batches, turning periodically to cook evenly, about 2 to 3 minutes per side.

YUCATÁN MARINADE
Makes about 1 1/2 cups

1/3 cup achiote paste

1/4 cup white wine vinegar

1/4 cup olive oil

1/4 cup freshly squeezed orange juice

1/4 cup pineapple juice

2 tablespoons finely diced yellow onion

1 teaspoon minced garlic

2 teaspoons salt

1/4 teaspoon white pepper

1 bay leaf

Place all the ingredients, except the bay leaf, in a blender or food processor and pulse until smooth. Add the bay leaf and use as directed.

Fajita Nachos

What makes these nachos so great—besides the tasty fajita-style steak or chicken—is the way they're built. Instead of dumping a bunch of stuff on top of a pile of chips, we start with whole, crisp Tortilla Flats, top them with beans, chicken or steak, and cheese like a mini-pizza, bake them, and *then* cut them into wedges. This way, you get a whole nacho experience in every bite.

1/2 cup diced red onion

1/2 cup minced cilantro

12 ounces shredded Cheddar

12 ounces shredded Monterey jack

12 6-inch Tortilla Flats (page 37)

4 cups Frijoles Refritos (page 34)

4 cups coarsely chopped steak fajitas (page 98) or chile-rubbed fajita chicken (page 97)

1 cup Everybody's Favorite Guacamole (page 39)

1 cup sour cream

1 cup Pico de Gallo (page 48)

4 Pickled Jalapeños (page 24)

4 cilantro sprigs

TO MAKE THE NACHOS: Preheat the oven to 350°. Combine the onion and cilantro in a mixing bowl and toss until they are evenly mixed. Set aside.

Combine the cheeses in a mixing bowl. Lay the Tortilla Flats on a baking sheet. Top with the beans, beef or chicken, and mixed cheeses, spreading each out evenly over the flats. Place the sheet in the oven and bake 4 to 5 minutes, or until the cheese is melted. Remove from the oven and cut each flat into 4 pieces.

TO SERVE: Sprinkle each piece with the cilantro-red onion mixture and place on a serving platter. (Spoon the guacamole, sour cream, and Pico de Gallo into mounds in the center of the chips. Garnish with the jalapeños and cilantro sprigs.)

Cut your nachos AFTER you've spread the filling on and heated them!

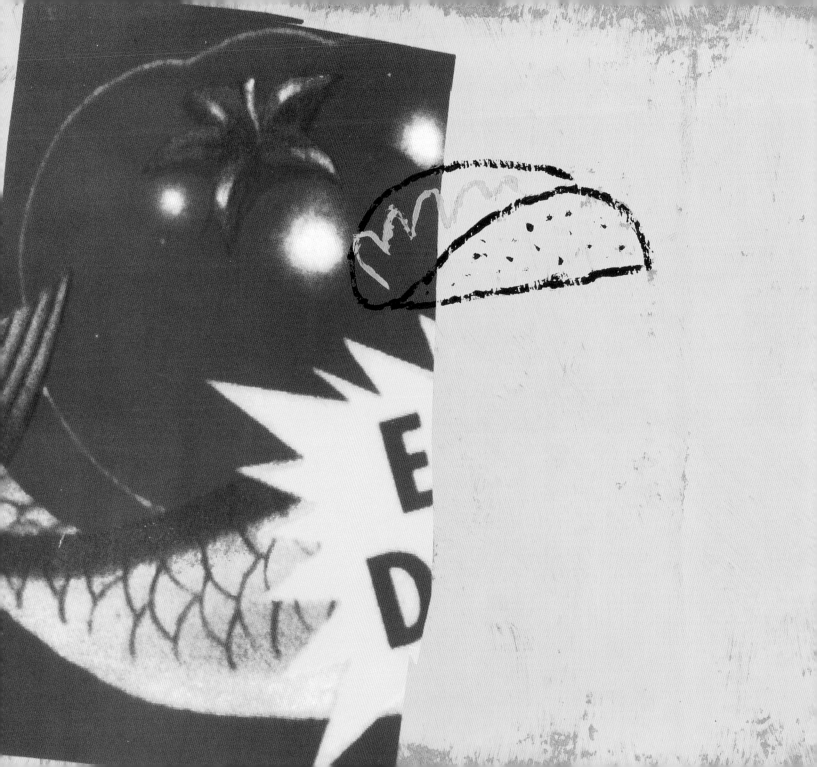

SOL FOOD

THE BEST TACOS, ENCHILADAS & TAMALES UNDER THE SUN

Holy Mole Chicken Enchiladas

Beer-Battered Fish Tacos

Shrimp & Potato Enchiladas Verdes

Cracked Crab Enchiladas

Chevys Three-Cheese Chile Rellenos

Classic Pork Tamales

Carnitas

Lemon-Herb-Chipotle Roasted Chicken

Margarita Scallops

Holy Mole Chicken Enchiladas

Serves 4 to 6

Our classic red mole sauce has got it all going on—it's rich, spicy, and nutty with a mysterious hint of chocolate lurking in the background for added intrigue. It makes amazing chicken enchiladas, and it's great for reheating leftover turkey (the traditional poultry of choice for mole) or chicken.

1/2 cup shelled pumpkin seeds

6 tablespoons sesame seeds

1/2 cup grated Ibarra chocolate

2 tablespoons water

4 cups New Mexico Red Chile Sauce, warmed (page 21)

1/2 teaspoon Chipotle Purée (page 26)

1 teaspoon ground cinnamon

1/2 teaspoon salt

1 tablespoon olive oil

2 pounds boneless, skinless chicken meat (from Homemade Chicken Stock, page 32), shredded

2 teaspoons chopped garlic

1 cup onions, chopped

2 cups chopped tomatoes

12 corn tortillas

Sour cream

1 avocado, thinly sliced

4 to 6 cilantro sprigs

TO MAKE THE SAUCE: Toast the pumpkin seeds and 4 tablespoons of the sesame seeds in a sauté pan over medium-high heat until lightly browned. Stir often to prevent the seeds from burning.

In the top of a double boiler over medium-low heat, combine the chocolate and water and melt until smooth. In a separate saucepan or in the microwave, heat the New Mexico Red Sauce. Combine half of the warm red sauce, the Chipotle Purée, pumpkin and sesame seeds, and cinnamon in a blender or food processor and purée. Add the puréed sauce and the chocolate mixture to the remaining red sauce and bring to a boil. Once boiling, decrease the heat to low and keep warm, stirring occasionally.

TO MAKE THE FILLING: Heat the olive oil in a large, heavy skillet over medium-high heat, sauté the chicken, garlic, and onions for 5 minutes. Add the tomatoes and sauté for another 5 minutes. Add 1 1/2 cups of the sauce, increase the heat to high and bring to a boil. Decrease the heat to low, and simmer for 20 minutes, stirring occasionally.

TO MAKE THE ENCHILADAS: Preheat the oven to 375°. Lay 6 of the tortillas on a baking sheet and place in the oven for 3 to 4 minutes to warm and soften them. (They can also be warmed for 30 seconds in the microwave.) Remove from the oven. Set a tortilla on your work surface and spoon about 1/3 cup of filling in a line down the center of the tortilla. Loosely roll up the tortilla and place in a 9 x 13-inch baking pan. Warm and fill the remaining 6 tortillas, adding them to the baking pan. Cover the enchiladas with the remaining 2 1/2 cups of sauce, and bake in the oven for 15 to 20 minutes, or until the enchiladas are warm throughout.

TO SERVE: Sprinkle the remaining 2 tablespoons of sesame seeds over the enchiladas. Garnish with a few dollops of sour cream, fanned-out avocado slices, and cilantro sprigs.

Beer-Battered Fish Tacos *Serves 4*

Beer and rice flour are all you need to make a perfect batter for fried fish. We like to use dark Mexican beer, but any kind with decent flavor will work. Rice flour is often sold in the Asian food section of supermarkets. Oh, and don't forget to serve these crispy fish tacos with the other five beers.

3/4 cup all-purpose flour

1/4 cup Fuego Spice Mix (page 23)

1 tablespoon salt

12 ounces Mexican beer

2 cups rice flour

Canola oil, for frying

3/4 pound sea bass, halibut, swordfish, or yellowfin tuna, cut into 4-inch-long strips

8 small flour tortillas (page 30)

Chipotle Sour Cream (see opposite page)

Smokin' Chipotle 'Slaw (page 33)

Pico de Gallo (page 48)

4 sprigs cilantro

TO BATTER THE FISH: Combine the flour, spice mix, and salt in a shallow bowl. In a separate bowl, combine the beer and rice flour. Dredge the fish fillets in the flour mixture and then dip in the beer mixture.

Line a platter with paper towels. Fill a heavy-bottomed skillet with 3 inches of oil. Heat over high heat until oil registers 350° on a candy thermometer. Drop 1 to 2 fillets at a time into the hot oil and deep-fry for about 2 minutes, turning once. Remove with a wire-mesh strainer, and transfer to the paper towel–lined platter to drain. Repeat until the other fillets are fried.

TO SERVE: Place 2 tortillas on each plate and fill with fish pieces, sour cream, slaw, and pico. Garnish each plate with a sprig of cilantro.

CHIPOTLE SOUR CREAM

Makes 1 generous cup

1/2 cup sour cream
1/2 cup mayonnaise
2 teaspoons Chipotle Purée (page 26)
1/2 teaspoon salt
1 tablespoon freshly squeezed lime juice

Combine all ingredients in a mixing bowl and stir with a whisk until smooth.

EL CAMARON

Shrimp & Potato Enchiladas Verdes

Serves 6 to 8

Here's one from our specials menu. And it's pretty special—soft corn tortillas rolled around a creamy, smoky shrimp-and-potato filling, baked in a tangy tomatillo green sauce.

1 tablespoon olive oil

1 1/2 cups diced
unpeeled potatoes

3/4 cup shredded Monterey jack

1/4 cup shredded Cheddar

2 teaspoons Chipotle Purée
(page 26)

2 tablespoons chopped cilantro

2 teaspoons salt

2 tablespoons butter

1 cup chopped yellow onion

3/4 cup stemmed, seeded, and
diced green bell pepper

1/4 cup stemmed, seeded, and
diced pasilla chiles

1 1/2 tablespoons chopped garlic

3 tablespoons flour

1 cup milk

12 ounces medium shrimp, shelled
and deveined

12 corn tortillas

2 cups Tomatillo Salsa Verde
(page 21)

4 to 6 ounces queso fresco

TO MAKE THE FILLING: In a sauté pan, heat the olive oil until hot and smoking. Add the potatoes in one even layer and allow to cook without stirring, 3 to 4 minutes. With a wooden spoon, gently stir the potatoes and cook for 2 minutes more. They should be browned and crispy. Place the sautéed potatoes on a paper towel–lined plate to cool.

In a separate mixing bowl, combine the cheeses, Chipotle Purée, cilantro, and salt and set aside.

Melt the butter in a small braising pan over medium heat. Add the onion, bell pepper, chiles, and garlic and sauté for 5 minutes. Mix in the flour and cook for 3 to 5 minutes, stirring frequently. Add the milk, using a whisk to thoroughly to incorporate it into the vegetable-flour mixture. Cook for 3 minutes, and then add the shrimp and cheese mixture. Cook for 3 more minutes, add the potatoes, and remove from the heat.

TO MAKE THE ENCHILADAS: Preheat the oven to 375°. Lay 6 tortillas on a baking sheet and place in the oven for 3 to 4 minutes to warm and soften them. (They can also be warmed for 30 seconds in the microwave.) Set a tortilla on your work surface and spoon about 1/3 cup of filling in a line down the center of the tortilla. Loosely roll up the tortilla and place in a 9 x 13-inch baking pan. Warm and fill the remaining 6 tortillas, adding them to the baking pan.

Cover the enchiladas with the salsa verde, and sprinkle the queso fresco over the top. Bake the enchiladas in the oven for 15 to 20 minutes, or until they are warm throughout.

Cracked Crab Enchiladas *Serves 6*

We're crazy about fresh crab. (Maybe it's our California roots.) And when crab's in season, you'll find it all over our menus. These enchiladas make a nice brunch entrée, served with a simple green salad on the side.

1 tablespoon olive oil

1/2 cup diced onion

1 teaspoon minced garlic

1/2 cup stemmed, seeded, and diced red peppers

1/2 cup chopped green onions

4 cups Chipotle-Cream Cheese Sauce (opposite page)

8 ounces Dungeness crabmeat

Salt and pepper

8 to 12 corn tortillas

1 1/2 cups queso fresco

TO MAKE THE FILLING: Heat the olive oil in a saucepan over medium-high heat. Add the onion and sauté until clear. Add the garlic, red peppers, and green onions and sauté for 30 seconds, or until soft. Add 1/2 cup of the Chipotle-Cream Cheese Sauce and bring to a boil. Remove from the heat and fold in the crabmeat. Season to taste with the salt and pepper.

TO MAKE THE ENCHILADAS: Preheat the oven to 375°. Lay 4 to 6 of the tortillas on a baking sheet and place in the oven for 3 to 4 minutes to warm and soften them. (They can also be warmed for 30 seconds in the microwave.) Set a tortilla on your work surface and spoon about 1/3 cup of filling in a line down the center of the tortilla. Loosely roll up the tortilla and place in a 9 x 13-inch baking pan. Warm and fill the remaining 4 to 6 tortillas, adding them to the baking pan. Cover the enchiladas with the remaining 3 1/2 cups sauce, and sprinkle the cheese over the top.

TO SERVE: Bake the enchiladas in the oven for 15 to 20 minutes, or until the cheese is melted and the enchiladas are warm throughout.

CHIPOTLE-CREAM CHEESE SAUCE

Makes about 2 1/2 cups

2 tablespoons butter

1/2 cup minced onion

1 teaspoon minced jalapeño

1 teaspoon minced garlic

1/4 cup minced red bell pepper

1/2 teaspoon minced fresh oregano

1/2 teaspoon salt

1/4 teaspoon ground cumin

1 teaspoon Chipotle Purée (page 26)

1 cup heavy cream

4 ounces cream cheese

1/2 cup grated Monterey

In a saucepan over medium-high heat, melt the butter. Add the onion and sauté until translucent. Add the jalapeño, garlic, and bell pepper and sauté until soft. Add the oregano, salt, cumin, and Chipotle Purée. Decrease the heat to low, add the cream and cream cheese, and simmer for 5 to 10 minutes. Remove the saucepan from the heat and stir in the jack cheese, stirring until melted and well incorporated. Keep warm over the lowest heat.

Chevys Three-Cheese Chile Rellenos

They may be a bit time-consuming, but there's nothing like 'em. Go for it.

1 1/2 cups shredded Cheddar

1 1/2 cups shredded Monterey jack

1 cup queso fresco, plus additional for garnish

6 eggs

1/4 cup flour plus 2 cups for dredging

8 poblano chiles, at least 5 inches long, roasted and peeled (page 27)

Canola oil

Ranchero Sauce (page 22)

TO MAKE THE RELLENOS: Combine the three cheeses in a mixing bowl. Cover and refrigerate.

Separate the eggs, placing the whites in a clean, dry mixing bowl and the yolks in a separate mixing bowl. (The bowl for the whites must be completely grease free and the egg whites must not have even the slightest bit of yolk in them in order to stiffen properly when whipped.) Using a handheld mixer on high speed, whip the egg whites until soft peaks form when the beaters are lifted up and out of the whipped whites. Add the 1/4 cup of flour and mix for 10 seconds. Add the reserved egg yolks and mix into the whites and flour, using medium speed, for 10 seconds. Using a large rubber spatula, finish incorporating the yolks by folding them in. Cover and refrigerate until ready to batter the rellenos.

Make a cut down the length of the chiles. Gently open chiles and hold under cold running water to rinse away the seeds. Pat the chiles dry with paper towels. Gently press about 1/3 cup of the cheese mixture into an oval-shaped ball and place inside one of the chiles. Using a wooden toothpick, "sew" the seam of the chile shut. Repeat until all the chiles are filled.

Place the flour on a plate. Gently roll the stuffed chiles in the flour to coat. Then dip the stuffed chiles in the egg mixture and coat completely. Line another plate with paper towels.

Fill a heavy skillet with 3 to 4 inches of the oil and heat over high until oil sizzles when a pinch of flour is dropped in. Add the stuffed chiles and fry one at a time. When the chiles are light golden brown, turn them to brown the other side. Remove the chiles from the hot oil with tongs and transfer to the paper towel–lined plate to drain.

TO SERVE: Place 2 rellenos on each plate and remove the toothpicks and discard. Spoon the Ranchero Sauce over the rellenos and sprinkle the cheese over.

THE PLATING GAME

WHEN IT COMES TO PRESENTING FOOD, we have a little motto: Do sweat the small stuff. Sure, the food's got to be fresh and delicious, but it's the goofy little details that make it fun.

CHIP SHAPES:
Fry up chips (page 36), using corn tortillas cut into shapes with cookie cutters. Use them to garnish beans, rice and other stuff. Hey! Don't stop at cacti! Think howlin' coyotes, stars, moons, sombreros.

SQUEEZE PLAY
Buy a plastic squeeze bottle. Fill it with El Ranch-O dressing (page 56), Chipotle Sour Cream (page 71), Roasted Red Pepper and Chipotle Chile Aioli (page 27) or sour cream, thinned with a splash of half-and-half. Now you're ready to garnish just about anything. And you'll be amazed at how cool a little squiggle can make even a burrito look. Top the squiggle with a spoonful of Pico de Gallo (page 48). Then stand back and bask in the glory.

A MINTY FRESH IDEA
We give away peppermints by the hundreds every day. Try it! They make people smile. Packets of Mexican gum have the same effect.

CORNY BUT COOL:
You know those dried corn husks in the Mexican section of your supermarket? Tear them into strips and serve a dollop of Sweet Corn Tomalito (page 36) or Everybody's Favorite Guacamole (page 39) on them. Tie them around silverware or napkins. Lay one on a plate and you've got yourself an instant Fresh Mex doily. How about party hats? Bowties? Hair ribbons?

SIX FLAGS OVER DINNER: check out your local party supply store and get some Mexican mini-flags. They go with just about everything.

BIG PLATES: Sure, you can serve food on any kind of plate. But buy some jumbo platters at a restaurant supply store. They're usually super cheap, and they give you lots of wide-open space to pile on the beans, rice, guac, and salsa.

THREE CHEERS FOR THE RED WHITE AND GREEN: Try "tricolor" plating and garnishing--like Pico de Gallo, sour cream and guacamole, or grilled red and green peppers with onion. You get the idea.

IT'S SPRIGTIME: A sprig of cilantro makes everything look nicer. Period.

how to roll
a tamale

FRESH MEX TIP #13

MASA MATTERS

The secret to really great homemade tamales is fresh masa--the dough made from dried corn cooked in limed water and ground into a paste. And the best place to get fresh masa is from a tortilla factory. If there's one in your town, chances are they'll sell fresh masa in tubs or bags. If not, you can buy it fresh (refrigerated) or frozen in some Mexican markets. And if all else fails, most supermarkets carry masa harina--a flour product made from dehydrated masa that you reconstitute with water.

Classic Pork Tamales *Makes 20 tamales*

Like chile rellenos, fresh tamales are special-occasion food. Invite some friends over to help make them. You won't have to twist anyone's arm to help eat them.

2 1/2 pounds pork shoulder or butt, cut into 2-inch cubes

2 tablespoons salt

5 cups New Mexico Red Chile Sauce (page 21)

1/2 teaspoon ground cumin

1/4 teaspoon cayenne pepper

4 cups (2 1/2 pounds) prepared masa

1/2 cup pork stock (reserved from cooking meat)

20 extra-large dried corn husks

1/2 cup queso fresco

TO MAKE THE FILLING: Place the pork in a large stockpot, cover with cold water, and add the salt. Bring to a boil over high heat, then decrease temperature to medium-low and simmer until tender, about 2 1/2 hours. The meat should fall apart. Strain the stock, reserving 1/4 cup for thinning the masa. Using a heavy-duty wire whisk, stir the pork, shredding it. With a spatula, gently fold in 2 1/2 cups of the red chile sauce and the cumin and cayenne. Cover and refrigerate until ready to assemble the tamales.

TO MAKE THE TAMALES: Place the masa in the bowl of a mixer. Add 1/4 cup of the pork stock, mixing on low speed until the liquid is incorporated. Mix on high speed until light and fluffy.

Soak all the corn husks in water until they are soft, about 20 minutes. Remove 1 husk from the water and pat dry. Lay the husk out on the work surface. Using a spatula or spoon, spread about 1/4 cup of the masa over the middle of the husk, leaving 1/2-inch borders along the sides, a 4-inch border at the top. Spoon 1/4 cup of filling down the center of the masa. Lift the sides of the corn husk up to meet each other in the center, and gently press to seal the masa together, making a tube shape that encases the filling. (The corn husk should wrap around the roll, but not be embedded in the masa or touching the filling.) Fold the top edge of the husk over the end of the roll. The tamale should be about 4 inches long and approximately 1 1/4 inches in diameter. Repeat until all the masa and filling are used. Cover the tamales with plastic wrap and refrigerate for 2 hours.

Place the tamales, folded end down, standing upright in a steamer insert in a large stockpot. Steam the tamales over boiling water for 15 to 20 minutes, or until the masa is firm and pulls away from the inside of the corn husks and the filling is heated through.

TO SERVE: Place the tamales (in their husks) on a platter and pass at the table with the remaining 2 1/2 cups of chile sauce. Sprinkle the queso fresco over all.

Carnitas

Serves 4 to 6

Traditional, taco stand–style, fork-tender pork, slowly simmered in a sweet and spicy marinade. Our top-secret ingredient (well, it was until now, anyway): Pepsi! Trust us, it's phenomenal. You can pile carnitas into warm flour tortillas, with guacamole, salsa, beans, and rice. Or serve it just like BBQ pork—it's even great at a picnic with soft rolls, potato salad, and corn on the cob.

3 pounds pork butt or shoulder

1 tablespoon Fuego Spice Mix
   (page 23)

1 orange, quartered

1 1/2 teaspoon chopped garlic

1 1/2 teaspoon ground cumin

1 teaspoon black pepper

1 cup Pepsi Cola plus additional,
   as needed

3/4 cup shortening

1 cup Agua Negra Marinade
   (page 98)

TO MAKE THE CARNITAS: Trim away the excess fat from the pork. (Remember to buy more meat in weight than you need, since you will trim some weight off in fat.) Cut the meat into 3-inch cubes. Dust the pork with the Fuego Spice Mix and press to adhere well.

Squeeze juice from the orange quarters into an airtight container. Add the peels. Add the garlic, cumin, salt, pepper, Pepsi, and marinade and mix to combine well. Add the seasoned meat cubes and marinate in the refrigerator overnight.

When ready to cook the meat the next day, remove from the marinade, and reserve the marinade. Meanwhile, place the shortening in a large, heavy skillet and melt over high heat. When the fat is smoking, add the pork and brown for about 15 minutes, turning occasionally. Add the reserved marinade and simmer for about 2 hours, or until the pork is tender and dark brown. As the meat cooks, add additional Pepsi to cover, as needed.

TO SERVE: Remove the meat from the skillet and chop into 3/4-inch pieces.

Lemon-Herb-Chipotle Roasted Chicken *Serves 6*

This spicy Mexican roasted chicken always turns out moist and memorable, thanks to two clever tricks: stuffing half a lemon inside the bird and spreading olive oil, garlic, and herbs under the skin. A little Chipotle Purée gives the outside extra flavor and a beautifully bronzed finish.

2 (2 3/4- to 3 1/2-pound) fresh whole fryer chickens

1/2 cup olive oil

2 tablespoons kosher salt

1 tablespoon black pepper

6 sprigs rosemary

6 sprigs oregano

1 lemon, cut in half

4 large garlic cloves, cut in half

2 tablespoons Chipotle Purée (page 26)

Butcher twine

TO MAKE THE CHICKEN: Preheat the oven to 350°. Remove the giblets from the body cavity, and trim away the excess fat. Rinse chicken inside and out under cold running water and pat dry.

Combine the olive oil, salt, and pepper in a small bowl. Coat the cavity of each chicken with some of the seasoned olive oil. Strip the leaves off 2 sprigs of rosemary and 2 sprigs oregano and mince; place inside the cavity. Place 2 each of the remaining sprigs of rosemary and oregano (leaves still attached) in the cavity.

Squeeze the juice from the lemon half into the cavity and place the half inside. Repeat with the other chicken. Truss the chicken drumsticks, closing the cavity. Or with a wooden skewer, pinch the skin together over the cavity and pierce through the skin and work your way up the body, "sewing" the skin together.

Spread the remaining seasoned olive oil under the breast skin. Place 2 garlic clove halves under the breast skin on each side. Strip the leaves off the remaining sprigs of rosemary and oregano and mince; distribute evenly under the breast skin. Sprinkle pepper and salt over the entire chicken. Baste the chicken with the Chipotle Purée.

Place the chicken on a roasting rack in a roasting pan and roast until the thigh juices run clear when the skin is pierced with a knife, 1 1/2 hours, basting with pan juices every 30 minutes, or until the thigh meat registers 165° on an instant-read thermometer. Remove from the oven and place on a chopping board.

TO SERVE: Using a cleaver or a chef's knife, cleave the whole chicken into quarters. Place one quarter on each plate and serve.

THE WHOLE ENCHILADA

Follow these formulas to make four more classic kinds of enchiladas.

ENCHILADA	FILLING +	SAUCE +	CHEESE
Chicken Enchiladas	salsa Chicken (page 32)	New Mexico Red Chile Sauce (page 21)	top with jack and Cheddar
Enchiladas Verdes	salsa Chicken (page 32)	Tomatillo Salsa Verde (page 21)	crumble queso fresco on top
Beef Enchiladas	Fajita Beef (page 98)	New Mexico Red Chile sauce	top with jack and Cheddar
Cheese Enchiladas	jack cheese and queso fresco	New Mexico Red Chile Sauce or Tomatillo Salsa Verde (page 21)	crumble queso fresco on top

ROLL YOUR OWN BURRITOS

Start with some Rio Bravo Red Rice (page 33) and homemade beans (pages 34 and 35), and you're halfway to building a bodacious burrito. To complete the process, add any of these fillings:

VEGGIES
San Antonio Vegetables (page 97)

CHICKEN
Salsa Chicken (page 32) or Fajita Chicken (page 97)

BEEF/PORK
Fajita Steak or Pork (pages 98 and 104)

EXTRAS
- Chipotle Sour Cream (page 71)
- Sweet Chipotle Dressing (page 26)
- Everybody's Favorite Guacamole (page 39)
- Salsa of your choice (pages 47 and 48)
- Smokin' Chipotle 'slaw (page 33)
- Pickled Jalapeños (page 24)
- shredded cheese
- shredded lettuce
- sour cream

Margarita Scallops

Serves 4

It happened like this: One of our chefs was relaxing after a shift, eating some scallops. A server walked by and said, "How about a Margarita with those?" Ping! Light bulb! Big idea! Ever since, we've served these seared scallops, sizzled in a savory "margarita" made with tequila, lime, and chiles.

1/4 cup tequila

1 cup freshly squeezed lime juice

1/2 cup freshly squeezed lemon juice

1/2 cup sugar

1 to 2 jalapeños, stemmed, seeded, and coarsely chopped (see tip, page 23)

3/4 cup 1/2-inch green onion pieces

1 cup chopped cilantro leaves

1 teaspoon garlic

1/2 teaspoon salt

1 pound large sea scallops

1 tablespoon olive oil

1 lime, quartered

3 teaspoons minced cilantro

TO MAKE THE SCALLOPS: Place all the ingredients, except the scallops and olive oil, in a blender or food processor and purée. Taste the mixture and add more jalapeño as desired. Transfer the mixture to a mixing bowl and set aside.

Rinse the scallops in cold water, and pat dry. In a nonstick sauté pan over high heat, heat the olive oil just until smoking. Add the scallops to the sauté pan and sear well without stirring or tossing. Add the citrus mixture to the pan, and bring to a boil. When the liquid reaches a boil, turn the scallops and cook for 1 minute more. Remove the scallops, cover to keep warm, and reduce the sauce to half its original volume over high heat.

TO SERVE: Divide the scallops among the plates. Pour the liquid from the pan directly over the plates. Garnish with the lime wedges and cilantro.

EL PESCA

CANTARIT

L CAMARO

THE TEQUILA EXPERTS

Tequila, lime, and salt. That might just be the tastiest Mexican flavor combo of them all. And the key is to begin with the best tequila you can get your hands on. Here's what you're looking for: Tequila is made from the fermented, distilled juice extracted from the roasted heart of the blue agave plant. Some tequilas are made from a blend of agave and sugar, but the super-premium ones are all made with 100% blue agave. How do you judge the quality of a tequila? For starters, check the grade:

Platas ("Silver") are the new kids on the block —aged less than 60 days.

Reposados ("Rested") are aged for 2 to 9 months for a smoother flavor.

Anejos ("Aged") are the top of the line. They're aged in oak barrels for at least 1 year or for as long as 6 years, and they're the darkest and smoothest tequilas of all. Bust out the snifters and go to town.

WILD BLUE YONDER: harvesting blue agave in Jalisco.

OAKY-DOKEY: traditional barrel aging makes the finest tequilas.

KEEP TASTING AND COMPARING.
Once you've found a tequila you love to drink straight up, then you've got the secret ingredient for some muy mouthwatering margaritas and tequinis (pages 42-45)—the Mexican martini invented at Chevys.

EAT A FAJITA

HOT OFF THE GRILL & READY TO WRAP

Chile-Rubbed Chicken Fajitas
Sizzlin' San Antonio Veggies
Mesquite-Grilled Steak Fajitas

Portobello & Asparagus Fajitas
Pork Loin Fajitas with
Apple, Onion & Bacon Sauté
Chile-Honey Glazed Prawns
Grilled Swordfish Steaks with
Mango Salsa

FRESH FAJITAS

THERE'S THIS THING THAT HAPPENS IN OUR RESTAURANTS EVERY DAY.

It's like a feeding frenzy. A server walks across the dining room carrying a platter of fajitas. First you hear the sizzle. Then you see the cloud of steam, and you get a whiff of that irresistible mesquite-grilled aroma. And suddenly, even though you were just planning to make a meal out of guac and chips, you're thinking, "I'd better go for the fajitas." You and about 15 other people.

That's the power of fajitas. And if it works at our place, there's no reason it can't work at yours. In fact, we think fajitas might just be the absolute best dinner party idea of all time. They've got something for everybody—tasty grilled meat and veggies, beans, rice, guacamole, and salsa all rolled up in warm flour tortillas. Plus, they're not just food. They're fun. Which is more than you can say about a pork roast.

SO HERE'S WHAT YOU DO. You make beans, rice, and all the trimmings. You marinate one or more kinds of meat. You chill a bunch of beers. You start the grill, and you set everything out on the table. When people show up, you let the brave ones roll out and griddle the tortillas, while you work the grill and engage in witty banter. When the grilling's done, you've got a Texas-sized spread that always turns out to be enough for about twice as many people as you invited. Try it. You'll see.

FOLLOW THESE EASY ASSEMBLY INSTRUCTIONS!

· Make a ton of beans (pages 34-35). Worst case scenario: you turn the leftovers into soup.

· Fix some Rio Bravo Red Rice (page 33). Figure 1/2 cup raw rice per person.

· Make at least one kind of grilled meat from this chapter.

· Homemade tortillas (page 30) are easier than you think. (Especially when you make the guests do half the work.)

· If you're not sure who eats what (and these days, who is?) Grilled Portobellos (page 103) are always a safe bet.

· It's just not a fajita without the Sizzlin' San Antonio Veggies (page 97).

· Guac it to 'em! Make a double batch (page 39) and set half out with some chips over by the beers.

· Make some Pico de Gallo (page 48), Tomatillo Salsa Verde (page 21), and Corn and Pepper Pico (page 48). Think of them as edible confetti.

· Set out some grated cheese, queso fresco, sour cream, chopped jalapeños, pickled jalapeños, etc. Fixin's for days.

· Whip up a batch of Sweet Corn Tomalito (page 36). Photocopy the recipe beforehand. At least one person will ask you for it.

Chile-Rubbed Chicken Fajitas
  atop Sizzlin' San Antonio Veggies with Pico de Gallo on the side

Chile-Rubbed Chicken Fajitas

This tender, spicy grilled chicken is just right in fajitas, not to mention quesadillas, burritos, taco, salads, and even sandwiches. Leftovers? Cut 'em into chunks and toss with a little mayo or Roasted Red Pepper and Chipotle Chile Aioli (page 27) and some diced jicama to make a memorable Mexican Chicken Salad.

2 pounds boneless, skinless
chicken breasts

2 cups Yucatán Marinade
(page 63)

2 tablespoons Fuego Spice Mix
(page 23)

TO MARINATE THE CHICKEN: Place the meat in a resealable container. Pour the marinade over the chicken, and move it around until it is evenly covered. Marinate in the refrigerator for 6 to 8 hours.

TO GRILL THE FAJITAS: Start the coals in a charcoal grill or preheat a gas grill. Remove the chicken from the marinade and coat it with the spice mix. Place the chicken on the grill and leave undisturbed until grill marks form, them rotate the meat 90° to create a second set of marks. After 3 to 4 minutes, turn the chicken and and cook the other side. Transfer the chicken to a work surface. Slice the chicken into 1/2-inch strips.

TO SERVE: Serve the chicken with all the recommended accompaniments (see page 94).

SIZZLIN' SAN ANTONIO VEGGIES

Makes 4 cups

2 tablespoons olive oil

2 cups thinly sliced yellow onions

1 tablespoon Fuego Spice Mix (page 23)

1 cup thinly sliced red bell peppers

1 cup thinly sliced green bell peppers

Heat a sauté pan over high heat. Add the olive oil and heat until the oil smokes. Add the onions and spice mix and sauté for 4 minutes. Add the peppers and sauté for about 2 minutes. Removed from the heat and serve immediately.

EL NOPAL

LA BANDERA

Mesquite-Grilled Steak Fajitas

Serves 4

Admit it. You're wondering what soy sauce is doing in a Mexican recipe. Well, sometimes "Fresh Mex" means looking at familiar things in a fresh new way. Besides being great on an egg roll, soy sauce is one of those secret ingredients that chefs use to wake up the flavor of all kinds of foods. Agua Negra is great for basic backyard barbecued steaks and chicken, too—just marinate 1 hour to overnight. These are the classic south Texas-style beef fajitas that put Chevys on the map: thinly sliced marinated flank steak rolled in a soft tortilla with all the fajita fixin's.

2 pounds skirt steak
Agua Negra Marinade (recipe follows)

TO MARINATE THE STEAK: Place the meat in a resealable container. Pour the marinade over the meat, and move the meat around to make sure that it is evenly covered. Marinate in the refrigerator for 6 to 8 hours.

TO GRILL THE STEAK: Start the coals in a charcoal grill or preheat a gas grill. Place the beef on the grill and leave undisturbed until grill marks form, then rotate the meat 90° to create a second set of marks. After 2 to 3 minutes, turn the beef to cook the other side. Transfer the beef to a work surface and slice.

TO SERVE: Serve the steak with all the recommended accompaniments (see page 94).

Makes about 3 1/4 cups

AGUA NEGRA MARINADE

1 cup soy sauce
2 cups pineapple juice
2 tablespoons ground cumin
1 1/2 teaspoons minced garlic
1/4 cup freshly squeezed lime juice

Combine all ingredients with a whisk in a mixing bowl, making sure to break up any lumps of spices. Store in an airtight container in the refrigerator for up to 2 days.

EL TAMBOR

CINCO DE MAYO

MARGARITAS FOR 3,000? No problema. Rio Bravo, Daytona Beach, Cinco '99.

INSTANT FIESTA: Add 4 mariachis; mix well.

At Chevys and Rio Bravo, every day is pretty much a fiesta. But once a year, we go totally loco for Cinco.

Cinco de Mayo, Spanish for "fifth of May," generally falls right around May fifth. It celebrates the defeat of the French at the battle of Puebla in 1862, and we think the best place to celebrate it is with us. We throw in everything but the kitchen sink-o. You know, mariachis, margaritas, piñatas, bobbing for jalapeños.

The party starts at around 11 a.m., and well, let's just say some people have been known to keep at it right on into Seis de Mayo.

THE PEPPER BOB: Like bobbing for apples. Only a lot more painful. Goggles required.

Portobello & Asparagus Fajitas Serves 4

One hundred percent meaty fajita satisfaction. Zero percent meat.

2 pounds portobello mushrooms, stems trimmed to 1/2-inch long

32 spears medium asparagus, trimmed to tips and 4-inch-long stalks

1 cup Sweet Chipotle Dressing (page 26)

1 cup roasted, peeled, seeded, and julienned bell peppers
  (page 27), warmed

TO GRILL THE VEGETABLES: Start the coals in a charcoal grill or preheat a gas grill. Marinate the portobellos and asparagus in the dressing while the grill heats up. Place mushrooms, stem side down, on the grill and grill about 2 minutes. Add the asparagus to the grill, and turn the mushrooms, cap side down, on the grill. Leave the mushrooms undisturbed until cross-hatch grill marks form, then rotate 90° to create a second set of marks. Transfer the mushrooms and asparagus to a work surface and slice the portobellos.

TO SERVE: Serve the vegetables with all the recommended accompaniments (see page 94).

FRESH MEX TIP #15

GRILL SKILLS

- When grilling both vegetables and meat, grill vegetables first, then keep them hot in the oven in a foil-covered pan while you grill the meat.

- Allow 6 to 8 ounces of raw meat, poultry, or seafood per person--this will yield cooked servings of 4 to 6 ounces.

- Trim most of the fat from red meat before grilling to avoid flare-ups.

- When grilling poultry, start it skin side down; it'll stick less, and the melting fat in the skin will "baste" the meat.

- After you take meat off the grill, cover it loosely with foil and let it sit for 5 to 10 minutes. It'll be juicier and more tender when you slice it.

Pork Loin Fajitas with Apple, Onion & Bacon Sauté

We serve our succulent Pork Fajitas with a little something extra: a warm relish of tart apples, bacon, and onions. If you like the tried-and-true combo of pork and applesauce, you'll like this even more. You can sauté the relish in advance, and it also makes a nice accompaniment to pork chops, roast pork, or turkey.

2 pounds boneless pork loin, cut into 4-ounce portions

Agua Negra Marinade (page 98)

Apple, Onion, and Bacon Sauté (recipe follows)

1/2 cup Sweet Hot Jalapeño Jelly (page 24)

TO MARINATE THE PORK: Place the meat in a resealable container. Pour the marinade over the pork and move it around until it is evenly covered. Marinate in the refrigerator for 6 to 8 hours.

TO GRILL THE PORK: Start the coals in a charcoal grill or preheat a gas grill. Place the pork on the grill and leave undisturbed until grill marks form, then rotate the meat 90° to create a second set of marks. After 4 to 5 minutes, turn the meat to grill the other side. Transfer the pork to a work surface and slice.

TO SERVE: Serve the pork with the apple-bacon sauté, spoonfuls of the jelly, and all the recommended accompaniments (see page 94).

APPLE, ONION, AND BACON SAUTÉ

Makes about 2 cups

2 Granny Smith apples

4 ounces bacon, cut into 1/4-inch-wide strips

1/4 cup sugar

1 white onion, cut in strips

1 large red bell pepper, stemmed, seeded, and julienned

1/2 teaspoon salt

2 tablespoons seasoned rice wine vinegar

Cut the apples into quarters, then core and slice 1/4 inch thick. In a large, heavy skillet, cook the bacon until almost crisp. Drain the excess grease. Add the sugar and cook until the sugar is brown. Add the onions and cook for 2 minutes. Add the sliced apples, red bell pepper, and salt, and cook for another 2 minutes. Add the vinegar to the pan and deglaze, scraping the bottom of the pan to dislodge any browned bits. Remove from heat and cool.

FRESH MEX TIP #16

MORE GRILL SKILLS

- We grill over mesquite charcoal. Always. If you're used to briquettes, give mesquite a try. It burns hotter, searing food quickly, and adds a clean, smoky flavor that's particularly good in Mexican cooking. If you've got a gas grill, check out mesquite chips.

- Marinate meat, poultry, or seafood in a resealable plastic bag. Fill the bag with meat and marinade, squeeze it to distribute everything evenly, press the air out of the bag, and seal. Lay the bag flat in a pan in the refrigerator, flipping occasionally.

- Don't use a marinade that's had raw meat in it as a sauce, unless you boil it for 5 minutes to kill any bacteria. Better idea: set aside some of the marinade before adding the meat to use as a sauce later.

- Slice flank steak, skirt steak, and other more fibrous meats across the grain at a 45° angle to the cutting board to create wide, thin strips that are tender to bite and easy to chew.

Chile-Honey Glazed Prawns

serves 4 to 6

If you do your skewering and glaze-making ahead of time, you can get these sweet, spicy grilled prawns on and off the grill in just a few minutes, which makes them a good choice for entertaining. Serve them over rice, give them the fajita treatment, or spear them individually and serve them right on the skewers as very cool hot hors d'oeuvres. The glaze gives a nice finish to fish, chicken, pork, or Cornish hens, too. Just brush it on during the last 5 minutes of grilling or broiling; watch carefully to avoid burning.

24 to 30 jumbo shrimp, shelled and deveined

1 cup Chile-Honey Glaze and Marinade (recipe follows)

12 to 18 bamboo skewers

Rio Bravo Red Rice (page 33)

TO GRILL THE SHRIMP: Start the coals in a charcoal grill or preheat a gas grill. Divide the glaze between two small bowls, setting one aside. Place the shrimp skewers on the hot grill. When they start to turn pink, turn and grill the other sides. When the shrimp are bright pink all over, after about 5 minutes total on the grill, baste with the glaze and remove from the heat.

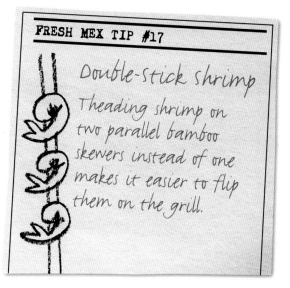

FRESH MEX TIP #17

Double-stick shrimp
Theading shrimp on two parallel bamboo skewers instead of one makes it easier to flip them on the grill.

TO SERVE: Place 6 shrimp on each plate. Spoon the remaining glaze over the shrimp. Serve over the rice or with recommended accompaniments (see page 94).

CHILE-HONEY GLAZE
AND MARINADE *Makes about 2 1/4 cups*

1 cup freshly squeezed orange juice

3/4 cup honey

1/3 cup freshly squeezed lime juice

1/3 cup Dijon mustard

2 tablespoons paprika

1 tablespoon chopped garlic

2 tablespoons chile powder

2 teaspoons oregano

2 teaspoons salt

1 teaspoon black pepper

1 teaspoon white pepper

TO MAKE THE MARINADE: Place all the ingredients in a blender and purée on high for 1 minute, or until smooth. Transfer to a saucepan and simmer over medium heat for 10 to 12 minutes, until thick and reduced by half.

Grilled Swordfish Steaks with Mango Salsa

The best fish-grilling advice we can give you is this: keep it simple. A light marinade and a few quick minutes over the fire are all it takes to make perfect fish that's seared on the outside and moist inside. If you're looking for more flavor, add it after the fact with a fresh salsa, a vinaigrette, or a dollop of aioli (page 27). And by the way, guacamole (page 39) is especially good with grilled swordfish.

1/2 cup olive oil

2 teaspoons minced garlic

Juice of 1 lime

1 tablespoon minced cilantro

1 teaspoon salt

1/2 teaspoon black pepper

4 fresh swordfish steaks
  (2 pounds total),
  1/2 to 3/4 inch thick

Mucho Mango Salsa (page 47)

TO MAKE THE SWORDFISH: Combine all the ingredients, except the swordfish and salsa, in a mixing bowl. Place the fish in a resealable container. Pour the marinade over the swordfish and move the fish around to make sure it is evenly covered. Marinate in the refrigerator for 6 to 8 hours.

Start the coals in a charcoal grill or preheat a gas grill. Place the swordfish steaks on the grill and leave undisturbed until grill marks form, then rotate the fish 90° to create a second set of marks. After about 4 minutes, turn the fish to cook on the other side for another cook 4 minutes, or until firm but still juicy.

TO SERVE: Place 1 steak on each plate and top with a generous spoonful of the salsa.

FRESH MEX TIP #18

Baja Grilled Fish Tacos
Fill flour tortillas with strips of swordfish and Mucho Mango salsa for a grilled fish taco alternative.

AZUCAR

SE hABLA
DESSERT

CUSTARDS, CARAMELS,
& OTHER SWEET SUPRISES SPOKEN HERE

Chocolate Tequila Bread Pudding

Cajeta

Flan in Two Flavors

Toffee Lace Tacos

Banana-Filled
   Chocolate Enchiladas

Chocolate Tequila Bread Pudding

Serves 6 to 8

You've found the one exception to our Fresh Mex philosophy: this decadent bread pudding actually works better with day-old bread, which is drier and soaks up more of the good stuff. It may be "stale Mex," but it tastes fantastic. Try it and see. The proof is in the pudding.

3/4 cup granulated sugar

1/2 loaf day-old French bread, cut into 1/2-inch slices, divided in half

2 tablespoons butter, melted

3/4 cup diced pineapple

3/4 cup chocolate chips

3 eggs, beaten

2 cups milk

1/4 cup tequila

1/4 cup Kahlua

1 tablespoon pure vanilla extract

1 cup heavy whipping cream

2 tablespoons granulated sugar

Cajeta Sauce (page 115)

Confectioners' sugar

TO MAKE THE BREAD PUDDING: Place the sugar in a saucepan over medium-high heat and cook, stirring occasionally, until the sugar melts and becomes a light golden color. (Do not let the sugar cook any longer; it will become bitter as it darkens.) Pour into a 9 x 9-inch ceramic or glass baking dish and tilt the pan to evenly coat the bottom and sides with the sugar. Let cool.

Line the pan with the bread slices and drizzle the melted butter evenly over the bread. Scatter the pineapple and chocolate chips over the top.

In a mixing bowl, whisk together the eggs, milk, tequila, Kahlua, and vanilla. Pour the egg mixture over the bread. Let stand at room temperature for 30 minutes, or until the bread has fully absorbed the liquid.

Preheat the oven to 350°. Set the baking dish in the oven in a large roasting pan. Fill the roasting dish with enough water to reach about 1 inch up the sides of the pan of pudding. Bake until the pudding is firm, about 50 minutes to 1 hour. If the bread is browning on the top too quickly (before the pudding sets), cover with foil. Remove the pudding from the oven and place on a cooling rack. Using a handheld or tabletop mixer, whip the cream and sugar until firm peaks form. Cover and place in the refrigerator until ready to serve.

TO SERVE: When the pudding has cooled for 20 to 30 minutes and is warm but not hot, cut into squares and place in shallow soup bowls. Spoon the Cajeta Sauce around the squares of bread pudding. Top each square with a dollop of whipped cream. Sift the confectioners' sugar over the desserts, lightly dusting the plates.

Cajeta *Makes 2 1/2 cups*

Cajeta ("Kah-HEH-tah") is one of Mexico's best-loved sweets—a golden caramel syrup made from sugar and milk. Making your own cajeta is a real experience—you get to watch everyday ingredients transform into something entirely different and incredibly tasty. And once you make it, you'll find a billion ways to use it, just like we do.

1 cup unsweetened flaked coconut
Cajeta Sauce (recipe follows)
1 quart vanilla ice cream

TO TOAST THE COCONUT: Preheat the oven to 350°. Spread the coconut on a baking sheet. Toast for 10 minutes, or until golden brown. Transfer to a plate and set aside to cool.

TO SERVE: Drizzle some of the sauce onto 6 dessert plates. Scoop 6 balls of ice cream, roll each in the coconut, and place over the sauce. Finish with a spoonful of the sauce over each scoop.

CAJETA SAUCE
1 quart milk
Pinch of baking soda
2 cups sugar
2 tablespoons cornstarch
1/4 cup cold water

TO MAKE THE SAUCE: Place the milk in a saucepan over medium heat. Stir in the baking soda, and heat until almost boiling. Add 1 cup of the sugar to the saucepan and stir until dissolved. Put the remaining 1 cup of sugar in a skillet over low heat and melt slowly, stirring continuously until the sugar is amber colored. (If the sugar is not browned enough, the flavor of the sauce will not be full and rich. If browned too much, it will turn bitter.) When the milk is boiling, add the caramelized sugar slowly, stirring continuously with a whisk. In a small bowl, dissolve the cornstarch in the cold water, stirring until completely smooth. Gradually stir the cornstarch mixture into the boiling milk. Continue to cook over low heat, at a slow, rolling boil, until the mixture thickens, about 30 minutes. Set aside to cool slightly.

Flan in Two Flavors *serves 4*

Along with Cajeta, flan is Mexico's other national obsession. And we're pretty "flanatical" about it, too. We make this recipe every night, using fresh eggs, whole milk, and pure vanilla extract. (Don't skimp on the vanilla; this is such a simple recipe, every flavor really counts.) For variety, go to "Flan B"—our light, creamy chocolate version.

1 3/4 cups sugar

1/2 teaspoon ground cinnamon

3 tablespoons water

3 cups whole milk

3 eggs

6 egg yolks

1 tablespoon pure vanilla extract

TO MAKE THE FLAN: Preheat the oven to 250°. In a large frying pan, heat 1 cup of the sugar and the cinnamon and caramelize over low heat (to prevent burning), stirring continuously until amber colored. Remove from the heat and slowly add the water while stirring. Immediately pour the caramelized sugar into four 8-ounce ramekins, swirling the cups to evenly coat the bottom.

Heat the milk in a saucepan over medium-low heat until almost simmering, then remove from the heat and set aside. Combine the eggs, egg yolks, remaining 3/4 cup sugar, and vanilla in a mixing bowl and beat with a whisk until pale yellow in color. Gradually add the hot milk while stirring continuously. Strain through a fine-mesh strainer.

Pour the custard batter into the ramekins, dividing equally. Skim any foam or bubbles off the surface of the custard. Place the ramekins in a roasting pan and fill the pan with 2 inches of warm water, so that the water comes about halfway up the outsides of the ramekins. Cover the ramekins with a sheet of parchment paper. Place the pan of custards in the oven and bake for 1 1/2 to 2 hours, or until a toothpick comes out clean when inserted in the middle of the flans. Cool to room temperature on a cooling rack, then cover and refrigerate overnight.

TO SERVE: Run a knife around the inside edge of the ramekins to loosen the flans. Gently invert and turn out the flans onto serving plates.

CHOCOLATE FLAN

To make chocolate flan, simply add 1 cup semisweet chocolate (chips or baking chocolate, broken into chunks) to the simmering milk. Stir until the chocolate melts and is evenly incorporated. Follow the recipe for plain flan to finish.

THROW A CINCO DE WHENEVER PARTY!

Hold the Mayo and have a Cinco-de-Whenever party in the middle of winter

If you ask us, the only thing wrong with Cinco de Mayo is that it only comes once a year. Can't wait for spring? Hey, don't stand on ceremony. Hold the "Mayo" and have a Cinco-de-Whenever party in the middle of winter!

FRESH MEX FINGER FOOD

· Fresh Tortilla Chips (page 36) with Everybody's Favorite Guacamole (page 39) and salsa (pages 47–48)
· Wings O' Fire (page 57)
· Red Chile Chicken Taquitos (page 54)
· Fajita Nachos (page 64)
· Yucatan Chicken Skewers (page 63)

CANTINA CHECKLIST

· Original Frozen Margaritas (page 42)
· Mango Margarita (page 42)
· Strawberry-Banana Margarita (page 42)
· Melonball Tequini (page 45)
· The Perfect Diez Tequini (page 45)
· Sea of Cortez Tequini (page 45)
· Washtub full of Mexican beers and sodas on ice

PARTY HAT

Fill the brim of a sombrero with chips. Then punch a dent in the center and nestle in a bowl of guac or salsa. No sombrero? No problemo. Just go to one of our restaurants and...uh...tell 'em it's your birthday.

DECOR ESSENTIALS

· Red, white, and green balloons
· Inflatable cactus
· Giant Mexican paper flowers
· Serapes. Lots of them.
· Mexican flags
· Sunlamp
· Seashells and sand
· Sunglasses

WHY NOT A PIÑATA?

Colorful. Interactive. And not just for kids any more. Especially if you fill it with something a little more interesting than penny candy. Like, say, individually wrapped chocolate truffles, PEZ® dispensers, paper flower petals, lottery tickets, fun fridge magnets, trendy pens, hip soaps, or a rubber chicken.

MUSICA!

Looking for toe-tappin' Cinco party tunes? Check out our staff's top picks pictured on the opposite page. Or, for an impromptu alternative, tune in to your local Mexican top-40 radio station and turn up the volume.

+

FIESTA!

Linda Ronstadt
CANCIONES DE MI PADRE
ASYLUM
9 60765-4

GIPSY KINGS
ELEKTRA
Musician
9 60845-4
ELEKTRA

Just Another Band From East L.A.
(LOS LOBOS featuring "LA BAMBA")

Mariachi Cobre
11095-4

Tito Puente
Oye Como Va —
the Dance Collection
2099

FRESH MEX MUSIC PICKS

GLORIA ESTEFAN
MI TIERRA
ET 53807
epic

BUENA VISTA SOCIAL CLUB
NONESUCH
79478-4

TEJANO ALL STARS
H4 72043 8
57391 4 9
EMI

Latin Dance Hits...
VARIOUS ARTISTS
NORTEÑO MIX
wea
the ultimate mexican party...
digalog
44010-4

Toffee Lace Tacos

Serves 4 to 6

Like our Chocolate Enchiladas, these crispy little "tacos" are total charmers. For a lighter alternative, fill them with fresh fruit (berries, nectarines, mangoes, or peaches are good choices), Cajeta (page 115), and a dollop of whipped cream.

3 pints fresh raspberries

1/3 cup confectioners' sugar

2 cups heavy cream

1 1/2 teaspoons pure vanilla extract

8 egg yolks

1 cup granulated sugar

12 Taco Shells (recipe follows)

TO MAKE THE RASPBERRY SAUCE: Place 2 pints of the raspberries and confectioners' sugar in a blender or food processor and purée until smooth. Set aside.

TO MAKE THE PASTRY CREAM: Heat the cream and vanilla in a large stainless steel saucepan over medium heat, slowly bringing the mixture to a boil. Meanwhile, place the egg yolks and sugar in a stainless steel (or other nonreactive) mixing bowl and whip with a handheld mixer until very shiny. Decrease the heat for the cream mixture to low, and slowly add the cream to the mixing bowl, whisking continuously. Return the cream-egg mixture to the saucepan and cook, whisking continuously, for 10 minutes, or until it is smooth and thick. Remove from the heat and cool completely, then cover and refrigerate.

TO SERVE: Divide the cold pastry cream among the cooled, firm taco shells, spooning the pastry cream directly down the center of the shells. Place a shell on each plate and drizzle the sauce over. Garnish the pastry cream in each shell with some of the remaining fresh raspberries.

TACO SHELLS

Makes 12

1 cup almonds

1/4 pound butter

1/2 cup sugar

2 tablespoons flour

2 tablespoons heavy cream

2 tablespoons grated Ibarra chocolate

TO MAKE TACO SHELLS: Preheat oven to 350°. Place the almonds on a baking sheet and toast for 6 to 8 minutes, or until golden brown and aromatic. Let cool, then finely grind in a food processor. (You should have 3/4 cup finely ground nuts.) Line the baking sheet with parchment paper. Cover 4 paper towel tubes with aluminum foil. Place all the ingredients in a saucepan and cook over low heat just until the butter melts and the ingredients are well mixed. Drop by tablespoonfuls onto the lined baking sheet. Bake the shells for 5 to 7 minutes, or until pale brown. Remove from the oven, cool for a few minutes, then shape the warm lacy circles into U-shaped taco shells, by laying them over the paper towel tubes. Let the shells cool draped over the tubes.

Banana-Filled Chocolate Enchiladas *Serves 6*

Alright, they're not really enchiladas. But these chocolate crepes with a banana-rum filling *are* really sensational.

1/2 cup butter

1/4 cup firmly packed brown sugar

3 tablespoons Myers's rum

4 ripe (not too speckled or black) bananas, chopped

12 Chocolate Crepes (recipe follows)

Chocolate Sauce (opposite page)

2 ounces white chocolate, shaved with a vegetable peeler or knife blade

6 large strawberries, stemmed and thinly sliced

4 to 6 mint sprigs

TO MAKE THE FILLING: Melt the butter and brown sugar in a saucepan over medium heat. Add the rum and chopped bananas, gently stirring to incorporate. Remove the filling from the heat and cool.

TO MAKE THE ENCHILADAS: Place 1 crepe on the work surface. Spoon about 3 to 4 tablespoons of banana filling down the center. Loosely roll up the crepe, like an enchilada, and place on a serving plate. Repeat until all the crepes are filled. Drizzle some of the Chocolate Sauce over the crepes. Garnish with the chocolate shavings, strawberry slices, and mint sprigs.

CHOCOLATE CREPES

2 tablespoons cocoa powder

1/2 cup all-purpose flour, sifted

2 large eggs

1/2 cup milk

1/2 cup water

2 tablespoons unsalted butter, melted

1/4 cup sugar

1/4 teaspoon salt

Heat a 10-inch nonstick skillet over medium heat. Spray once with vegetable oil cooking spray. Pour 3 tablespoons of crepe batter into the hot pan. Lifting and tilting the pan, quickly coat the whole pan bottom with batter before it cooks. Place the pan back on the heat and cook undisturbed for 45 seconds to 1 minute, or until the batter looks dry in the pan. Using a spatula, loosen one side of the crepe. Carefully lift the crepe out of the pan with your fingers and flip it over. Cook for 1 minute more and remove from the pan onto a plate. Repeat with the remaining batter, stacking the crepes on the plate. When the finished crepes are cool, cover tightly with plastic wrap until ready to use.

CHOCOLATE SAUCE

Makes about 2 cups

1/2 cup milk

2 tablespoons sugar

2 tablespoons light corn syrup

2 tablespoons water

6 ounces bittersweet chocolate, chopped

1 tablespoon vanilla extract

Pinch salt

Combine the milk, sugar, and corn syrup in a saucepan over high heat, and bring to a boil. Turn off heat and add the chocolate, submerging it in the hot liquid. Let stand until melted, and then whisk the sauce to blend well. Add the vanilla and salt. Set the sauce aside until it has cooled to room temperature, then cover and refrigerate.

Index

Index *Continued...*

ACKNOWLEDGMENTS
The list of people who helped us make this book
is long enough to fill another book, so we'll just keep it simple
and say thanks to all the creative folks (you know who you are!)
who played a part in bringing the Fresh Mex Cookbook to life.
Fresh Mex® is more than food, it's an attitude and a way of life.
Our employees bring Fresh Mex® to life every single day. And for
that, we tip our sombreros to them.

SOURCES FOR SPECIALTY INGREDIENTS
Most of the ingredients called for in our Fresh Mex® recipes
can be found at farmer's markets, gourmet retail shops,
Mexican markets, and well-stocked general markets.
For those items not stocked by these retailers, we recommend
you try the following:

Dean & Deluca
Catalog Department
560 Broadway
New York, NY 10012
800/221-7714
www.deandeluca.com

Coyote General Store
132 W. Water St.
Santa Fe, NM 87501
800/866-4695

Melissa's
www.melissas.com
800/588-0151